# SENIOR CARE IS BOOMING!

*Own a Profitable Senior Care Company*

## by

# ANTHONY NELSON

# TABLE OF CONTENTS

# CHAPTER 5 – Hands on Marketing

Marketing to Senior Housing Assisted Living, Independent Living, & Skilled Nursing Facilities

Definitions

Setting the appointment

The appointment

Presentation to Independent Living & Assisted Living Centers

Presentations to Skilled Nursing Facilities & Rehabilitation Centers

Marketing to Home Health and Hospice Agencies

Definitions

Setting the Appointment

The presentation

# Other books authored by Anthony Nelson

*Clean Up in the Cleaning Business*

*Senior Care is Booming!*

*The Property Preservation Coach*

*Start A Yard Care Company*

*Dedicated to every person willing to risk everything to be successful!*

# ABOUT THE AUTHOR

I am an entrepreneur, author and business owner.  I have helped many people realize their dream of business ownership.  My wife Jennifer and I are the founders and owners of SHS Franchising.  SHS Franchising is the parent company of Spectrum Home Services.  Spectrum Home Services is a very successful home services franchise.

My introduction to the service industry was in 1984 as an 18 year old "kid" running for city council in my hometown of Westminster, California.  You are probably asking what running for a political office has to do with marketing a small business.  Well, you would be surprised by the similarities between the two.  When you run for office you have to get your name out in the community by sending out mailers and postcards and you have to put up signs and billboards.  During my campaign, I knocked on over 20,000 doors and introduced myself to thousands of prospective voters.  Like most new small businesses, I had a very small budget and was an unknown entity.  Even though I lost that election, I only lost by less than 100 votes!  Not so bad for an 18 year old kid with little money or political clout.

In 1991, I moved to Utah and I obtained my Real Estate license and began selling Real Estate.  Once again, I found myself in the same predicament that I had found myself in 1984 running for city council.

I was the new Realtor on the block and because I had just moved to the state, I had absolutely no base of friends or clients to call upon. I had to hit the phones and pound the streets to generate my first listing and buyer. I sold Real Estate successfully for 10 years before getting the itch to start my own business.

In 2000, my wife and I started Spectrum Home Services. Spectrum Home Services is service business like no other. The idea for Spectrum Home Services actually came from a Masters project my wife had completed to get her Masters degree in Physical Therapy. The business plan was developed to provide seniors with an alternative to the standard home care companies that only provided companionship services.

As a Physical Therapist, my wife knew that seniors needed more than just someone to play cards with them and go to the store, if they wanted to stay out of a nursing home and live at home as long as possible. The plan was to provide seniors with handyman, cleaning, yard, and home care services under one company that would help them stay safe in their home. As a Realtor, I also saw a need for a convenient way to order these same services for my clients.

We opened our first office in Salt Lake City in the winter of 2000 and quickly began to grow. After years of rapid growth, we decided to franchise the concept. Spectrum Home Services now has over 30 offices in 20 plus states and we are still growing.

This book is designed to help you start a small business and chase your dream of success. While I am a strong believer in the franchise industry and concept it is not always the right choice for everyone. Competition is good! A vibrant small business community is the back bone of our great country and anything that helps promote small business ownership is a benefit for the future.

# INTRODUCTION

Welcome to the Senior Care Business!

The trend in senior care services will continue to experience an upward spiral in demand as baby boomers age. In 2001, the first of the baby boom generation reached what used to be known as retirement age. For the next 18 years, boomers will turn 65 at a rate of about 8000 a day. As this unique generation grows older, they will transform the government institutions and businesses that serve them.

Many other companies recognize this trend as well. You will have competition, so it is important that you have a "value added proposition". Some of your value added services could include 24 hour care, meal preparation, deep cleaning, yard care services and handyman services. It is important that your senior care business provide quality services at a competitive price.

Everyone says that customer service separates them from their competition. That is something that is a necessity to stay alive in the service industry. So instead, I would like you to ask yourself what services you offer to your customer that will separate you from your local competition.

Most franchise senior care companies have a much higher fixed overhead! This overhead can come in the form of a required outside office, higher royalties, national ad fees, call center charges, proprietary software charges and a huge local advertising budget including a required large display ad in the yellow pages. Because of their higher fixed overhead, you can beat them on price and maintain your profit margins!

What you are looking for is a nice steady recurring revenue stream for you. Your business is not looking to have hundreds of one time customers. Next, I will give you the tools that will assist you in starting and operating a successful senior care business in the chapters that follow.

# CHAPTER 1

# OPERATIONS

## Definitions

### Home Making

Home making is a service which is directed by the client or client's family. It may involve cleaning but often involves other "chores" which the senior is aundry, meal preparation, running errands, making beds etc. Most clients expect the homemaker to engage the client in conversation to help them stay oriented and involved in activities. Homemaking is usually done 2 to 3 times a week for 2 or 3 hours at a time depending on client needs.

### Companionship

When providing companionship the focus is entirely on the client. Usually the family has directed the companion in activities the client may enjoy. Playing cards, taking a walk, reading and reminiscing over old photographs are a few of the activities that can be provided. Clients that require companionship often cannot be left alone due to confusion or poor health. If the client is resting or wants to be alone, the companion can perform any homemaking tasks that will not upset the client.

Companionship is often provided when a family member needs a break and performing a few simple chores really makes a big impact on the care giver.

Companionship hours vary significantly. Some clients are seen weekly for 2 to 6 hours, others are seen every day. If you are seeing a client more than 20 hours a week on an ongoing basis the client should pay 2 weeks in advance and be billed at least every 2 weeks. Keep in mind the financial resources of the client as this volume of care gets expensive quickly. Once the client is spending more than $200/day on care it is no longer cost effective to keep them at home. However, the client and family is the customer and our job is to provide what they need in the home as long as it is safe.

**Personal Care**

This is a service that involves touching a client and is performed by a personal care aide, personal attendant or Certified Nursing Assistant (CNA) depending on state regulation. Personal care aides help clients get out of bed, bathe, dress, and groom. In many states this particular type of assistance is regulated and must be performed under a special license. Many companies provide companionship for 24 hours at a time but do not employ personal care aides. Your company should require that if your employees are regularly assisting the clients with personal care activities they must be a personal care aide.

**Environmental Adaptation**

Handyman services will vary significantly when the customer is a senior or disabled client. The focus is on safety and accessibility. Installing grab bars and removing shower doors can allow a client to remain in their own home rather than going to an institution. With assisted living ranging from $1,000 - $4,000 a month, most home modifications are worth a try. Handymen are required to follow the guidelines established by Americans with Disabilities Act (ADA) when building ramps on homes where there is public access (front door).

There is a great deal of research and interest in how home modifications can reduce the cost of health care. Across the country money is being put into home modification programs and there are not many vendors applying to participate in these programs. This funding is discussed under Block Grants.

## Management and Office Functions

Your objective is to train employees that are versatile and can effectively anticipate and meet client needs. As defined above the staff must be able to change focus as the client's needs change. A good senior services manager can partner the client's needs to the employee that is best suited to meet those needs. Also, realize that not every client employee relationship is going to work. The manager needs to be able to change staff to keep the customer happy when necessary.

The office staff will receive customer requests by direct phone call, internet leads or referral companies. Most of the time getting back to the customer quickly is critical in winning the opportunity to provide services. Too many steps in the referral process can reduce your chance to win business. The office must be able to quickly reach the senior services supervisor, or must be able to schedule an initial visit.

## Answering the Phone/ Courtesy calls

Most phone scripts begin the same way, "(Your Company Name), this is *** how may I help you?" (or something similar) Many times with senior care the customer is looking for information. "Do you offer bathing, companionship, meal prep etc? Rather than simply stating yes we offer those services try to understand the callers story or situation. "Yes we offer bathing, tell me what's going on." The more you empathize and understand the client or family needs the better you will be able to match services and a care giver to meet those needs.

Most of the time the customer is price shopping and wants an hourly rate. Try not to just give rates over the phone. You will not have the lowest rate and you may lose the sale. If they are persistent about a rate try and educate them a little if possible.

All rates vary depending on the needs of the clients and skills of the employee. Let the customer know if any hands-on care is needed the rate should go up, as the level of skill is higher. Many of your competitors will have a 4 hour minimum. Let the client know if they only need an hour or two they will still pay for the full 4 hours.

Be sure the person answering the phone has a consistent method of tracking information and scheduling appointments. The best approach to the above scenario is, "Could I have a staff member come out and meet with you, so we can match our services to meet your needs and budget?" Finally, if they do not want a staff member to come out and continue to insist on a price, give them a range and encourage them to ask questions about minimums and employee skill level as they shop around. It is also good to refer them to a competitive partner for a price comparison. If they are looking for 24 hour care and you do not provide 24 hour services, refer them to the agency you like to work with. Then be sure you make a phone call or at least send an e-mail to let the agency know you sent them a referral.

## Setting in-home estimate appointments

Once you have the opportunity to visit a client in their home the chances of closing the sale are much better. Listen to the customer's issues and remember to address **their** needs. Be sure the senior care employee meeting with the customer takes good notes. If they are interested in meal prep focus on how to best meet that need first. Do you have staff to cover the hours and skills the client needs?

Once you determine the client is appropriate determine which is the most convenient days or times to schedule the visits set up the first visit while you are there if possible. If the client is apprehensive you may have to agree to have them meet the staff before the visit, or preferably the senior care employee may go with the staff member on the first visit to make introductions

If the client requires assistance you cannot provide, it is good to have other companies you can refer to. I would recommend that you have at least one personal care agency if the client requires 24 hour care and one skilled nursing company if the request of the client appears skilled to refer the clients to if you decide not to provide those services. If your staff is unsure if they can provide the services it is best to make a referral, or have a nurse on contract that can make the assessment for your staff.

### Tracking work flow

There are many scheduling programs out there that can assist you with your scheduling of clients. I would recommend that you do research on programs that will meet the needs of your scheduling requirements. Also, make sure that if you are using QuickBooks that it merges seamlessly so there is no double entering client information.

## Paperwork

### Current Customers

Each customer will have a permanent file with the original intake form, service agreement and current care plan. See Chapter 10.

If this is a private pay client and you are providing personal care you may also need an LPN or RN signature/ screen and a notice of privacy form signed. The senior care supervisor or lead CNA will do the original intake and should bring this information to the office. The employee will need a copy of the care plan, to be educated on the customer's needs and priorities, and may need to be introduced to the client. In some cases a copy of the paperwork is kept in a folder in the client's home, (if multiple agencies are visiting, supervision is spotty or the client is confused.) The employee should have a binder to keep the client information as well as a supply of work order forms. Each visit the "work order" is added to the customer file.

It is always necessary to keep a hard copy file for audits and in case of emergency. Most states require these client files to be kept for 5 to 7 years.

- Estimates done, but "did not close" book. You will have this information in your scheduling program. Your estimates done but "did not close" book should include your copy of the original estimate.
- Former Customers book. Move current customers out of the current customer book into this book when they cancel services. You will often get call backs to re-start the service. (If the client dies, remove them from your database) Use the "did not close" and former customer data bases for marketing campaigns.

In your scheduling program, each "team" or employee should have a calendar with their visits for that day/week. These are usually printed at the end of the week for the following week. Employees need to drop off their signed work orders as proof they visited the client. These forms are put in permanent, hard copy files and must be kept for 5 to 7 years depending on your state requirements.

After the client is visited, the information is moved into billing. The work orders are checked against the employee's time sheet and employees are paid for the visits they completed with a signed work order.

## Other Considerations

**Courtesy Calls**

Place Courtesy Calls the day before the visit to your clients. It's a great customer service tool and it will cut down on your cancellation rate. Occasionally these clients have doctor's appointments or other engagements and you cannot provide services to the client if they are not home. Calling ahead gives you the chance to reschedule the appointment without sending staff to an empty house. It also allows you to bring additional equipment and supplies if the client mentions a special need.

When possible do not give the client a specific time you can be there. Mid morning-early afternoon are usually specific enough. If you give them an exact time such as nine o'clock they will be expecting the employee at 8:55 and will begin calling the office. Have the employee call the office if they are running late so the office can notify the client. This helps keep track of your staff and prevents the clients from getting the employees cell phone numbers.

**Equipment**

- Gloves
- Blood pressure cuff and stethoscope
- (Gown, mask and goggles – only for infection control clients)

# CHAPTER 2

# PERSONNEL

## Employee vs. Independent Contractor

Independent contractors and employees are not the same, and it's important to understand the difference. Knowing this distinction will help you determine what your first hiring move will be and affect how you withhold a variety of taxes and avoid costly legal consequences.

## What's the Difference?

### An Independent Contractor:

-Operates under a business name

-Has his/her own employees

-Maintains a separate business checking account

-Advertises his/her business' services

-Invoices for work completed

-Has more than one client

-Has own tools and sets own hours

Keeps business records

**An Employee:**

-Performs duties dictated or controlled by others

-Is given training for work to be done

-Works for only one employer

Many small businesses rely on independent contractors for their staffing needs. There are many benefits to using contractors over hiring employees:

-Savings in labor costs

-Reduced liability

-Flexibility in hiring and firing

**Why Does It Matter?**

Misclassification of an individual as an independent contractor may have a number of costly legal consequences.

-If your independent contractor is discovered to meet the legal definition of an employee, you may be required to:

-Reimburse them for wages you should've paid them under the Fair Labor Standards Act, including overtime and minimum wage

-Pay back taxes and penalties for federal and state income taxes, Social Security, Medicare and unemployment

-Pay any misclassified injured employees workers' compensation benefits

-Provide employee benefits, including health insurance, retirement, etc.

## Tax Requirements

Visit the IRS Independent Contractor or Employee guide to learn about the tax implications of either scenario, download and fill out a form to have the IRS officially determine your workers' status, and find other related resources.

## Employment Information

There is no single test for determining if an individual is an independent contractor or an employee under the Fair Labor Standards Act. However, the following guidelines should be taken into account:

-The extent to which the services rendered are an integral part of the principal's business

-The permanency of the relationship

-The amount of the alleged contractor's investment in facilities and equipment

-The nature and degree of control by the principal

 The alleged contractor's opportunities for profit and loss

-The amount of initiative, judgment, or foresight in open market competition with others that is required for the success of the claimed independent contractor

-The degree of independent business organization and operation

Whether a person is an independent contractor or an employee generally depends on the amount of control exercised by the employer over the work being done. Read Equal Employment Opportunity Laws - Who's Covered? For more information on how to determine whether a person is an independent contractor or an employee, and which are covered under federal laws.

## Employees

### Recruiting

Employees will be your biggest challenge in any service-based businesses. Don't let it stop you. Your future employee is out there now either not working or working.

Most of the usual employment search engines work well for personal care aides. Your state department of work force services is a good source for employees looking for work. You may also try posting a tear off ad in laundry mats, apartment complexes or churches. Advertisements in papers that are free will work as well. For general labor stay away from newspapers that cost money as well as search engines that cost, your employees are not likely to pay to find a job.

For those working, many are already in some form of health care; home health, skilled nursing, assisted living or personal care agencies. Since these companies are also hiring you may approach them and determine if they had applicants they chose not to hire. Many times they will give you the information on their second and third choice. (In the future if you run an advertisement you may share your candidates with one of these agencies.) You may interview them to see if they are good candidates. Not only will they have personal care aides, if they are an institution they often have candidates that applied for cleaning positions.

Often employees in this industry work more than one job. Always get permission from the administrator or person in charge of human resources before you approach employees of any work place. Approach the human resource person and let them know you are interested in offering part time employment to a few of their employees. Let them know their company is always considered primary and you will not pursue full time employment. They may already know employees that are looking for additional work.

Every area has training centers where people interested in providing personal care services can be trained. Usually they are based in community colleges or private agencies. (Some nursing homes train their own aides but only for their employees.) The training centers are an excellent source of potential employees. Let the training staffs know you are looking for employees that are willing to clean as well as provide personal care services. Make regular contact with the agencies, especially around graduation. (The best personal care aids start as cleaners/home makers It is far less difficult to train a cleaner to provide personal care then the other way around.) With that thought in mind you may send a cleaner to "school" to become a personal care aide. Usually you make friends with the school by sending your own employees there and may get future employees from them.

## Interview Questions

To find out if the employee is a good fit you need to know what they want from the job. If they have a hard time being flexible or working with people homemaking may not be a good fit. You are looking for employees that enjoy care giving and preferably have had some experience as a caregiver.

## Pay Structure & Hourly Average

The sad irony is that the private cleaning usually pays much better then homemaking or personal care.

It is not possible to set up homemaking or companionship as a piece rate. Usually the client needs someone with them for a specified number of hours on a regular basis. You can justify a more expensive rate however, by providing a better quality product.

Pay your employees more to get better employees and charge the clients more. Also, be sure the employees understand they should be looking for opportunities to provide extra services. Cleaning, meal prep, laundry etc are always needed. If the client is sleeping or involved in their favorite program for a certain amount of time the employees need to provide extra services during that time. The client must be charged at least 2 to 3 times the employees wage. If you charge less than that you will not be able to cover your office overhead. If the employee makes $10/hr you must charge $25-$30/hr. don't be discouraged if you hear of competition providing services for $18 - $20/hr. Remember, they often have a four hour minimum and may not be using certified professionals.

**Initial Training**

Have a formalized training session you are putting your new employees through. If you have the capability to develop a training video have them watch the training video, fill out ALL of the appropriate paperwork and set up an employee file.

-Application

-Job Description

-Federal and state withholding

-I-9

-Acknowledgement of Employee Handbook

-Non-Compete agreement

-Authorization for a Background check

-Uniform Receipt

Be sure to have a way to contact your employees and a way for them to contact the office. Discourage using the client's phone.

Once you are up and going, identify a training team and send your new employees out to be trained by them. Give your training team a small stipend for doing this. They will let you know if you have the "right" employee.

**Employee Tips**

It would be great to have a small break area where everyone can congregate in the morning. Route Managers can get their keys, client sheets, route books and stock equipment and refresh supplies.

I highly recommend setting up a continental breakfast for your employees, if this is feasible. Just some simple things like coffee, bagels, margarine, jelly and peanut butter. It also goes a long way when the boss passes out paychecks on Friday mornings. It is also a good day to have a short staff meeting.

Other tips:

-Always recognize birthdays and service anniversaries!!!! A certificate on the wall, a birthday card and cake go a long way!

-Always ask for input from your field staff and reward and recognize implemented ideas.

-Take away any us vs. them mentality that sometimes exists in this industry.

## Company Expectations

The key attribute of a successful organization is being "results-oriented". A valuable employee or contractor is able to act according to the circumstances, pursue the results, neither postponing the solution of issues nor multiplying bureaucracy.

**Other corporate standards should include:**

-Professionalism — to possess unique and up-to-date knowledge and have the capability to apply this knowledge; one's own competent vision and opinion; as well as the capability to achieve results.

-Initiative — to make proposals on new projects, optimize functions and business processes; show desire to participate in project and work groups; and contribute to performance improvement.

-Responsibility — to achieve results within the set timeframe; to be ready to bear responsibility for failure to fulfill duties; to effectively balance personal objectives/results and the objectives/results of the company.

-Resourcefulness and capability to find non-routine solutions — to be internal entrepreneurs of the job functions or business based on either a new combination of Company, generating new solutions and projects outside the range of standard duties, traditional approaches and processes or their non-standard application.

-Loyalty — involvement in the activities of the company and its brand; avoidance of destructive negative criticism and readiness to participate in solution of company problems. All employees and managers are obliged to use company assets only for improvement and development of your company. Group's business and not for self-profit or individual career promotion.

-Focus on cooperation with fellow employees — readiness to participate in cross-functional teams and projects; giving positive and effective response to the requests of co-workers from other company divisions; readiness to share information. Efforts to establish barriers between divisions, competition for information and status, influence on functional divisions, sabotage of requests and appeals shall be considered destructive activity.

## Duties and Responsibilities/Job Descriptions

The following are job descriptions for employees that your company may need to hire. It is very important that your employees understand their job descriptions and what is expect of them.

## Office Manager

**GENERAL JOB DESCRIPTION**: Main goal is to provide exceptional customer service to all clients and to adhere to job duties and company polices. The position will be responsible for all clients and employees.

**CONSULTS WITH**: Owners, employees, vendors, and clients

**REPORTS TO**: owner/operator or appointed supervisor.

**JOB RESPONSIBILITIES**:

**Customer Service**
- Maintain a professional appearance, adhering to dress code

- Address all incoming telephone calls from prospective and existing clients, owner/operator in the field, etc. Taking and delivering messages as necessary.
- Working with the public in a courteous and efficient manner to ensure client satisfaction
- Practice excellent client service and ensures employees are doing the same
- Address client complaints and problems
- Make follow-up calls to maintain relationships with clients and referrals
- Monitor quality control and ensures services are completed as needed
- Adheres to written instructions from owner/operator or appointed supervisor
- General Office
- Possess a comprehensive knowledge of general computer knowledge and Microsoft Office Products.
- Maintaining files
- Generating reports
- Submits weekly sales reports for royalties to SHS on time
- Responsible for the overall cleanliness of the office

- Complete Medicaid billing

- Reconcile MFS checks for contractors

- Input all invoices into QuickBooks; cleaning, yard, handyman, MFS

- Receive payments in QuickBooks

- Input payroll information into QuickBooks

- Calculate piece rate pay on all work orders

- Reconcile work with payment, keep track of collections at time of service and billing

- Collecting from customers as needed

- Send monthly statements to Real estate agents, Guardians, Senior Care agencies, and any other agencies as needed

- Check MFS daily to get new work orders

- Monitor employees and ensure jobs are being completed properly and on a timely basis

- Train, supervise, and motivate employees in daily operations

- Bill credit cards

- Arrange for maintenance and/or repair work as necessary for the vehicles, equipment, etc

- Make sure all employees are adhering to safety and security procedures

- Schedule employees to complete cleaning, yard jobs
- Upload MFS data as needed
- Other duties as requested
- Required Qualifications
- At least 18 years of age
- Knowledge of computers and Microsoft Office Products
- Good Interpersonal Skills
- Willing to Give and Receive Feedback
- Typing speed of 45 wpm
- Standards
- Clients always come first, and their needs will be met unless there is a conflict with the needs of other clients or the business as a whole
- Employees should not work under the influence of mood-altering or illegal drugs or alcohol
- Neat appearance, adherence to the dress code and good personal hygiene are expected

# Administrative/ Office Assistant

### Duties:

- Answer Phones

  (Customer service, inform clients about services offered, etc)

- Mail

  (Sort through and open mail, Make sure mail gets distributed to the appropriate person)

- Input "Payables" into quick books

  (Any bills that the company needs to pay must be entered and accounted for in quick books)

- Invoicing for both cleaning departments

  (Elite and home cleaning)

- Run credit cards

  (For clients that received services)

- Receive payments

  (From clients and put them into quick books)

- Cleaning staffs payroll/ Time clock

  (Make sure time clocks are updated and the cleaning staff is getting paid appropriately)

- Filing

  (Keep a well organized office by making sure all paperwork is filed correctly)

- First contact for bids

  (See description below on how this is to be done)

- Support for management

  (Help keep the office running efficiently and effectively by doing various other tasks assigned by management)

- Medicaid Billing

**Personality Traits**:

Customer Service Driven, Team Attitude, Multi Tasker, Organized, Efficient, Task Oriented

**Experience**:

Office Experience, Administrative Experience, Experience In A Support Role, Basic Computer Knowledge

# Supervisor

**GENERAL JOB DESCRIPTION**: Main goal is to provide exceptional customer service to all clients and to adhere to job duties and company polices. The position will be responsible for all cleaning and senior care clients and employees.

**CONSULTS WITH:** Owners, employees, vendors, and clients

**REPORTS TO**: Owner, Office Manager

**JOB RESPONSIBILITIES**:

- Assist _____ in ensuring all aspects of the Mission Statement, Business Plan, Sales and Financial goals are met in the department.
- Increase Housekeeping and Senior Care revenue as planned in Quarterly / Yearly Plan
- Increase Profit Margin as planned in Quarterly / Yearly Plan
- Increase Housekeeping and Senior Care Clients as planned in Quarterly / Yearly Plan
- Maintain expenditures to within budget guidelines

**Training**

- Plan and implement the pre-training checklist with new employees
- Plan and implement an ongoing training/safety program that meets (Your Company Name) and government standards
- Plan and implement quarterly training/safety meeting with all division Managers.

**Departmental Scheduling & Billing**

- Utilize scheduling program in all aspects of your day to day operations
- Schedule all Daily/weekly work assigned to department
- Ensure all department customers are invoiced professionally and on schedule

- Order and Track Department Literature, Supplies & Equipment
- Maintain and Update MSDS sheets as per federal guidelines for the department
- Ensure all "tools" required for department are in supply and issued in appropriate quantities.
- Eliminate product waste and miss-use
- Track all company equipment and maintain a "custody" form for all teams
- Manage Maintenance of Department Equipment
- Set up a maintenance program for all department equipment
- Work with Field Service Manager to implement your maintenance program

**Marketing & Bids**

- Maintain a minimum 85% closing rate for department bids
- Market to "customer rich" locations on a regular basis
- Implement a 5 – 5 – 10 door hanging program
- Implement a "leave behind" program for department
- Know and mingle with the "competition"
- Plan "Seasonal" advertizing and marketing programs

**Employee Recruiting**

- Maintain a pool of perspective employees / employees in training

- Use all available medias to advertize for potential employees
- Work with the other managers to conduct first interviews for perspective employees
- Pick and train an employee that could be your vacation relief supervisor

## Customer Satisfaction

- Be the "Face" of (Your Company Name)
- Maintain our 100% satisfaction guarantee policy
- Call 25% of our customer base each service to ensure satisfaction
- Know EVERY customer and their "hot buttons" and document them

## Quality Control

- Personally inspect a minimum of 25% of our clients homes each month
- Divide inspections equally between teams
- Understand the weaknesses of each team and eliminate them (the weakness)

**Whatever else may be asked of you by _____.**

# Personal Care Aide

- Performs all duties outlined in the client's service agreement.
- Reports directly to the owner/operator or appointed supervisor.
- Demonstrates competency in all areas of training for personal care.
- Maintains a minimum of six hours of in-service training per year.
- Adheres to written instructions from owner/operator or appointed supervisor.
- Assists clients with the following:

## Housekeeping

- Performing Grooming and Dressing
- Helping with eating
- Preparing Meals
- Helping with oral hygiene and denture care
- Helping with toileting and toilet hygiene
- Arranging for medical and dental care, including transportation to and from the appointment
- Taking and recording oral temperatures
- Administering emergency first aid
- Providing and Arranging for Social Interaction

- Arranging for Transportation

**Required Qualifications**

- At least 18 years of age

- Trained in CPR

- Must be a Certified Nursing Assistant

- Good Interpersonal Skills

- Willing to Give and Receive Feedback

**Standards**

- Clients always come first, and their needs will be met unless there is a conflict with the needs of other clients or the business as a whole.

- Employees should not work under the influence of mood-altering or illegal drugs or alcohol.

- Neat appearance, adherence to the dress code and good personal hygiene are expected.

## Homemaker

**GENERAL JOB DESCRIPTION**: Main goal is to provide exceptional customer service to all clients and to adhere to job duties and company polices. The position will be responsible for all Homemaking clients and employees.

**CONSULTS WITH**: Owners, employees, vendors, and clients

**REPORTS TO**: owner/operator or appointed supervisor.

**JOB RESPONSIBILITIES:**

- Customer Service
- Perform all duties outlined in the client's service agreement.
- Meet customer's needs end to end
- Maintain a professional appearance, adhering to dress code
- Adheres to written instructions from owner/operator or appointed supervisor
- General Homemaking
- Housekeeping
- Doing Laundry
- Preparing Meals
- Running Errands
- Providing and Arranging for Social Interaction
- Arranging for Transportation

**Miscellaneous**

- Demonstrates competency in all areas of training for homemaking
- Maintains a minimum of six hours of in-service training per year
- Look for ways to improve process and reduce cost
- Other duties as requested by the Owners

**Required Qualifications**

- At least 18 years of age
- Trained in CPR
- Good Interpersonal Skills
- Willing to Give and Receive Feedback

**Standards**

- Clients always come first, and their needs will be met unless there is a conflict with the needs of other clients or the business as a whole
- Employees should not work under the influence of mood-altering or illegal drugs or alcohol
- Neat appearance, adherence to the dress code and good personal hygiene are expected

# Yard Care Specialist

**GENERAL JOB DESCRIPTION**: Main goal is to provide exceptional customer service to all clients and to adhere to job duties and company polices. The position will be responsible for all Yard Care clients and employees.

**CONSULTS WITH**:  Owners, employees, vendors, and clients

**REPORTS TO**:  owner/operator or appointed supervisor.

**JOB RESPONSIBILITIES:**

## Customer Service

- Perform all duties outlined in the client's service agreement.
- Meet customer's needs end to end
- Maintain a professional appearance, adhering to dress code
- Adheres to written instructions from owner/operator or appointed supervisor

## General Homemaking

- Able to lift 75-100 lbs
- Valid driver's license
- Able to operate yard and snow machinery
- Fertilizing
- Miscellaneous
- Demonstrates competency in all areas of training for homemaking
- Maintains a minimum of six hours of in-service training per year
- Look for ways to improve process and reduce cost
- Other duties as requested by the Owners

## Required Qualifications

- At least 18 years of age

- Trained in CPR

- Good Interpersonal Skills

- Willing to Give and Receive Feedback

- Standards

- Clients always come first, and their needs will be met unless there is a conflict with the needs of other clients or the business as a whole

- Employees should not work under the influence of mood-altering or illegal drugs or alcohol

- Neat appearance, adherence to the dress code and good personal hygiene are expected

# House Cleaner

**GENERAL JOB DESCRIPTION**: Main goal is to provide exceptional customer service to all clients and to adhere to job duties and company polices. The position will be responsible for all clients and employees.

**CONSULTS WITH**: Owners, employees, vendors, and clients

**REPORTS TO**: owner/operator or appointed supervisor.

**JOB RESPONSIBILITIES**:

- Customer Service

- Able to work quickly with quality results

- Able to cross sell other services when opportunities arise

- Performs all duties outlined in the client's service agreement
- Reports directly to office manager
- Always gives outstanding customer service
- Demonstrate competency in all areas of training for cleaning position
- Able to follow instructions, make decisions and ask for help as necessary.
- Must have a current driver's license, reliable transportation and clean driving record.
- Able to pass drug screening and background check.
- Ability to follow company dress code and represent the company in a professional manner
- Able to do or have the knowledge of the following:
- Knowledge of current cleaning methods, cleaning solutions, shop vacuum, regular vacuum and proper floor care.
- Knowledge of cleaning and maintenance safety practices.
- Ability to multi-task.
- Detail oriented.
- Able to prepare cleaning materials and solutions for each job as needed.
- Be aware of choosing the proper tools and cleaning agents as needed.
- Able to communicate with supervisor and other employees.
- Able to read signs, labels and work instructions.
- Plan and complete assigned duties in allowable time.
- Preparing and accepting paperwork for billing.
- Able to use and care for company products and equipment.

- Accept forms of payments from customers: checks and credit cards only.

**Able to have the ability to do the following duties on the cleaning site:**

- Sweep, scrub, dust, vacuum and mop floors.
- Spot clean carpets as needed.
- Clean walls, baseboards, window sills and blinds.
- Dust furniture, pictures, lights, fans and other fixtures as needed.
- Clean inside and outside of cabinets.
- Clean bathrooms, toilet, sink, shower/tub, light fixtures, cabinets, mirrors and floors.
- Wipe down all kitchen appliances, cabinets, including inside of microwave, oven and refrigerator.
- Inspect and remove any cobwebs found.
- Wipe down light switch plates in each room.
- Operate washer and dryer.

**Required Qualifications**

- At least 18 years of age
- Good Interpersonal Skills
- Willing to give and receive feedback

**Standards**

- Clients always come first, and their needs will be met unless there is a conflict with the needs of other clients or the business as a whole.

- Employees should not work under the influence of mood-altering or illegal drugs or alcohol.

- Neat appearance, adherence to the dress code and good personal hygiene are expected.

# CHAPTER 3

# GOVERNMENT AGING SERVICES PROGRAMS

## Overview of the program

In 1965 Medicare and Medicaid were enacted as Title XVIII and Title XIX of the social security act, extending health coverage to almost all Americans aged 65 or older.  Medicaid is the largest program providing medical and health-related services to America's poorest people.  There are 5 broad coverage groups: Children, Pregnant Women; adults in families with Dependent children; individuals with disabilities, and **individuals 65 or over.** For more information see www.longtermcarelink.net (guide to eldercare planning) (Medicaid and Long Term Care)

In 1977 The Health Care Financing Administration (HCFA) was established to administer the Medicare and Medicaid programs.  This agency was later re-named Centers for Medicare & Medicaid Services (CMS) This Federal agency serves as the focal point for developing, interpreting and evaluating laws, regulations and policies that govern financial operation and management of the Medicare & Medicaid programs.

Within broad national guidelines which CMS provides, each of the states; establishes its own eligibility standards; determines the type, amount, duration, and scope of services; sets the rate of payment for services; and administers its own program.

## Area Agency on Aging (AAA)

In 1973 the Older Americans Act established the Area Agencies on Aging (AAA) to respond to the needs of Americans aged 60 and over in every local community.

The AAA's are in charge of administering the funds that are used for the individuals 65 and older who qualify. Because there are several levels of interpretation, each Area Agency on Aging (AAA) may have slightly different rules or emphasis. For instance, in a state with many elderly such as Florida the income level required to receive services may be set much lower than in a state with fewer elderly.

To assist individuals in understanding regulation and eligibility, in 1991 the National Association of Area Agencies on Aging (NAAAA) established the Eldercare Locator. This is a toll-free 800 number for identifying the information and referral services provided by State and Local Area Agencies on Aging. More recently the NAAAA joined the Alliance of Information and Referral Systems (AIRS) to help develop a more comprehensive information and referral network known as 211. For more information please log on to http://211us.org

AAA services fall into five categories:

1. Information and access
2. Community based services
3. In-home services
4. Housing
5. Elder Rights

## Information and Access

- Information and Referral/assistance – a source for locating services available from an AAA agency or another service agency in the community

- Health Insurance Counseling – helps beneficiaries understand their options and rights under Medicare and Medicaid and obtain information on Medigap and other insurance alternatives

- Care Management – a review of an individual's social, psychological and physical health challenges, resulting in a "plan of care" for services or treatment, if appropriate

- Transportation – rides to critical destinations such as a doctor's office or the grocery store.

- Caregiver Support – education and resources that enable caregivers to provide care for an older family member while maintaining their own quality of life

- Retirement Planning and Education – help for older adults as they prepare for their retirement, with a focus on issues such as pensions, health concerns, legal issues, and work and leisure options.

## Community Based Services

- Employment Services – a way to help the individual find meaningful work, including assessment, testing, job counseling, education and placement

- <u>Senior Centers</u> – a gathering place where older adults can enjoy social, physical and recreational activities. Senior centers may serve as congregate meal sites
- <u>Congregate Meals</u> – group meals served at senior centers, schools and other sites for the purpose of providing a nutritious meal in a social environment
- <u>Adult Day Care Service</u> – a community based group program designed to meet the needs of functionally impaired adults and provide respite for their caregivers
- <u>Volunteer Opportunities</u> – a way for healthy older adults to continue to contribute to their community

## In-Home Services

- <u>Meals on Wheels</u> – mid-day and evening meals delivered to individuals who cannot shop or prepare their own meals, often by a volunteer who also provides a sense of security and social contact to a homebound individual
- <u>Homemakers</u> – assistance with tasks essential to maintaining a household, such as grocery shopping and housekeeping
- <u>Chore Services</u> – a step beyond homemaking – includes minor home repairs, yard work and general home maintenance
- <u>Telephone Reassurance</u> – regular, pre-scheduled calls to homebound older adults to reduce isolation and provide a routine safety check
- <u>Friendly Visiting</u> – periodic neighborly visits to homebound older adults to provide social contact and reassurance

- <u>Energy Assistance and Weatherization</u> – payment of fuel bills and home weatherization for low income people

- <u>Emergency Response Systems</u> – electronic devices which allow individuals to contact a response center in the case of an emergency, such as a fall

- <u>Home Health Services</u> – a variety of services including skilled nursing care, health monitoring, dispensing of medication, physical and other forms of therapy, and instructing individuals and family members about home care

- <u>Personal Care Services</u> – assistance with bathing, feeding, walking and other daily activities

- <u>Respite Care</u> – a break for family members from care giving responsibilities for a short period of time

## Housing

- <u>Senior Housing</u> – housing designed to accommodate the needs and preferences of independent older adults

- <u>Alternative Community-Based Living Facilities</u> – a range of housing facilities that bridge the gap between independent living and nursing homes, such as assisted living and adult foster care.

## Elder Rights

- <u>Legal Assistance</u> – advice and counsel for older persons and their families faced with financial and legal concerns

- Elder Abuse Prevention Programs – designed to alleviate situations of abuse, neglect or self-neglect; includes programs such as adult protection and guardianship/ conservatorship
- Ombudsmen Services for Compliant Resolution – ombudsman investigate and when possible, resolve complaints made by or on behalf of older adults who are residents of long-term care facilities

Many AAA programs are consistent across the nation, for example, Meals on Wheels, Ombudsman Program, and Transportation. Recently, new programs have been added in many areas to address the changing needs of this growing population. The AAA's realize their dollars go farther in programs that offer care giver support and many alternatives to nursing home placement are available.

## Payor Sources

### Medicaid Aging Waiver

This program offers in-home and community based services, sometimes abbreviated (HCBS) to individuals age 65 and over who would need nursing facility care without help. The client must be at or below poverty level to receive Medicaid. Each client receives a Case Manager to assist them with the program eligibility process and a long term plan of care. This program is different from the state Medicaid program because it uses special deduction guidelines to assist elderly persons to become eligible for Medicaid and the additional benefits of the Aging Waiver. These guidelines allow seniors with higher incomes to also qualify for these needed services. Not every state participates in the

Medicaid Aging Waiver. Most states do participate and provide the following services;

- Personal Care Services (Home health aide or personal care attendant)
- Homemaking services (may include shopping, meal preparation, assistance with medical appointments, laundry, cleaning and errands etc.)
- Chore Service
- Transportation Services
- Emergency Response System
- Medication Reminder System
- Adult Day Care Services
- In-Home Caregiver Respite
- Nursing Home Overnight Caregiver Respite
- Home Delivered Meals
- Companion Service
- Medical Equipment – limited
- Home Modification – limited
- Caregiver Training Assistance

Usually a visit to your local AAA is necessary to find out what programs are offered, what they are called and how to apply. What you want to participate in are Home and Community Based Services (HCBS) programs.

**Alternatives Programs and Block Grants**

Some states have additional programs which are funded by federal, state and/or county funds. These programs are an "alternative" to nursing home placement and are sometimes called alternatives programs. They may also be referred to as HCBS or HCBA programs and they may cover all of the above services or just a select few. For example in Salt Lake County they have The Alternatives Program (TAP) which covers all of the above services for people with too much money to qualify for Medicaid but who are financially unable to afford to pay full price for needed services. Without TAP most of these approximately 500 clients would be in nursing homes. This would cost the state over $60,000 per client, per year! For this reason the community has been very active in keeping the funding of this program available.

In addition to the Alternatives program, States may have several block grants available. Block grants are sums of money set aside for a specific purpose. To be eligible to participate in Block Grants you usually must complete a Request For Proposal (RFP) to describe how you will be able to meet the needs of the program. If you become aware of an RFP for a program in your area, contact the main office for assistance.

Recently, some counties have put out an RFP for Environmental Adaptation programs. This is a Community Services Block Grant (CSBG) for home modifications. The funds allow companies like yours to bid and provide handyman services for clients to modify their homes. Clients are senior or disabled and the projects may include wheelchair ramps, removing shower doors, pulling the tub and building a roll-in shower, widening doorways, etc.

**Caregiver Support Program**

The National Family Caregiver Support Program (NFCSP), established in 2000, provides grants to States and Territories, based on their share of the population aged 70 and over. The grants are designed to fund a range of supports that assist family and informal caregivers to care for their loved ones at home for as long as possible.

The government has realized that families are the major provider of long term care and care giving exacts a heavy emotional, physical and financial toll. Since almost half of all caregivers are currently over age 50 and one-third describe their own health as fair to poor, the graying of America is not only stressing the formal health care system it may destroy the informal system as well. The NFCSP offers a range of services to support family caregivers. Under this program, States shall provide five types of services:

1. Information to caregivers about available services
2. Assistance to caregivers in gaining access to the services
3. Individual counseling, organization of support groups and caregiver training
4. Respite care
5. Supplemental services, on a limited basis

These services work in conjunction with other State and Community-Based Services to provide a coordinated set of supports. Studies have shown that these services can reduce caregiver depression, anxiety, and stress and enable them to provide care longer. This helps avoid or delay the need for costly institutional care. To find the contact in your area, log on to www.aoa.gov this is the administration on aging website. Under programs, click on home and community based long term care, then click on National Family Caregiver Support Program. The program is explained and there is a link at the bottom to the eldercare locator which is the best way to determine who in your community administers this program. Request information on becoming a provider and let them know you can provide chore service, handyman service, housekeeping, and companionship. If you are providing personal care, let them know that as well.

**Veteran's Aid & Attendance Program**

This program is a monthly pension benefit offered through the Department of Veterans Affairs (VA) for Veterans and their spouses over the age of 65. The program is designed to help clients who have in-home care or live in nursing-homes or assisted-living facilities. To qualify clients must be in need of regular personal assistance due to physical or mental disability not acquired during war. This program is for Companies that provide personal care. The pension is determined by adjusting for un-reimbursed medical expenses from the veteran's or surviving spouse's total household income. If the veteran is earning $1000/month, an aide just 3 hours 3 times a week will cost approximately $900/month. As mentioned earlier a few hours several times a week can add up very quickly. Some of these hours must be used for personal care; however additional services that your offers can help make up the difference in qualifying clients for this program.

## Long Term Care Insurance

Most long term care companies are outsourcing their referrals. Companies such as Nations Care Link send the referral on behalf of the insurance company to the service company such as yours. To participate you need to complete an application and agree to a standard rate for reimbursement. These programs contact you by e-mail or phone to place the client with your service. Traditionally they contact a provider and you have a limited amount of time to get back to them with a staffing solution. If you cannot staff the need they will call the next provider. Please do not sign up for this referral program until you have staff available? If you cannot staff a few cases in a row you will be dropped from their provider list.

## Workman's Comp

If a person suffers an injury at work their services are paid for through Workman's Compensation Fund. These may be administered through the state or through a private company. Start with the person you write your monthly check to. Ask who is in charge of "case management" and try to set up an appointment to visit them. When possible present your services to as many case managers as you can.

This organization has the potential to refer everything from homemaking to complete home remodel and room additions. In most cases they pay ½ down and ½ at the completion of the job. If it is state funded and you are asked to go out of your area they will compensate for mileage and in some cases room and board depending on the size of the job.

## Guardian & Conservator

More and more it is becoming common for families to seek the assistance of a financial conservator to help manage the finances of one or more of their parents. If families are in crisis and care management is initiated the first step is to get someone in control of the money. A conservator is appointed by the court and is responsible to the court for how the money is spent. In some states this person must hold a license such as an attorney or social worker, however most states require no special training. Elder care conservators should be familiar with the programs and assistance outlined previously. It makes sense to many families to assign a conservator especially if the children do not live near their parents and are worried about them falling prey to a scam.

## Duties of a Conservator

A conservatorship can be set up after a judge decides that a person (called the "conservatee") can't take care of themselves or their finances. Then the judge chooses another person or organization (called the "conservator") to be in charge of the conservatee's care or finances, or both.

## Information:

The court can say you are:

- The conservator of a person,
- The conservator of an estate, or
- Both.

When the court chooses you as a conservator, you are responsible to the court. You take on certain jobs and responsibilities. The court can examine everything you do as a conservator.

## The Conservatee's Rights

A conservatee does not lose all rights. They can still have a say in important decisions. They have the right to:

- Be treated with understanding and respect;
- Have their wishes considered; and
- Be well cared for by you.

In general, conservatees keep the right to:

- Control their own salary;
- Make or change their will;
- Get married;
- Get mail;
- Have a lawyer;
- Ask a judge to change conservators;
- Ask a judge to end the conservatorship;
- Vote, unless a judge says they're not able to;
- Control personal spending money if a judge says they can have an allowance; and
- Make their own health-care decisions, unless a judge gives that right to a conservator.

**Conservator of the Person**

When the court chooses you as the conservator of a person, this means you:

- Arrange for the conservatee's care and protection;
- Decide where the conservatee will live; and
- Are in charge of:
    - health care,
    - food,
    - clothes, personal care,
    - housekeeping, transportation, and
    - Recreation.

**Figure out what the conservatee needs:**

You must figure out what the conservatee needs and how to meet those needs.

**Decide where the conservatee will live:**

You can decide where the conservatee will live. But you must choose the least restrictive place. It has to be appropriate, safe, and comfortable for the conservatee. And it has to let the conservatee be as independent as possible.

Often the conservator is not in charge of the person rather the estate

When the court chooses you to be the conservator of an estate, you will:

- Manage the conservatee's finances;
- Protect the conservatee's income and property;
- Make a list of everything in the estate;
- Make a plan to make sure the conservatee's needs are met;
- Make sure the conservatee's bills are paid;
- Invest the conservatee's money;
- Make sure the conservatee gets all the benefits he or she is eligible for;
- Make sure the conservatee's taxes are filed and paid on time;
- Keep exact financial records; and
- Make regular reports of the financial accounts to the court and other interested persons.

Following these guidelines it is easy to see why a conservator would like to work with (Your Company Name). We can assist with almost all of a client's needs in one company. We provide all of the services a client would need to stay safe in their home, we can adjust services as their needs change and we can relocate the client if necessary.

Financial advisors, CPA's, attorneys and social services all have "conservator" listings. For an outline of the fiduciary process see appendix?

**Grants**

To participate in the bid process you may have to become registered through one of the internet bidding sites. Recently more and more AAA organizations are going to an online bid system to assure all interested and eligible parties have a chance to bid on the program.

- To find out about the bid sites used in your area go to www.aptac-us.org/new and determine who your local representative is. While this is not mandatory these relationships can get you into local networking opportunities in your community.
- You must obtain a DUNs number. Go to http://fedgov.dnb.com/webform this process takes about 48 hours. This is a free service although some sites try and get you to "upgrade" for a fee, the upgrade is not necessary
- Next register for Central Contractor Registration (CCR) @ http://www.ccr.gov this takes about an hour to complete and you have certification within about 48 hours
- Next register for ORCA @ http://orca.bpn.gov this takes about 1 hour to complete
  During the registration process you will need the following codes

NAICS Codes

561720    janitorial services

561730    landscaping

484210    Moving

236118    Residential remodel

624120    Services for elderly


SIC Codes

7349 cleaning

0782 mowing


Once you have completed the registration process and have your DUNs, ORCA and CCR you can register on the sites used in your area. The most common sites are; fedbizops.com, bidsync.com and bidnotice.org. If you find additional sites please let the main office know.

# CHAPTER 4

# ADVERTISING YOUR SENIOR CARE BUSINESS

## INTRODUCTION

The advertising strategy that you develop for your company needs to achieve the maximum name recognition and consumer acceptance..

This section of the book will provide you with information on marketing and selling, covering such topics as prospect identification and sales techniques. It also provides guidelines and procedures for developing and implementing an advertising program in your market that will effectively promote your business.

Advertising dollars, if well spent, offer a high rate of return for a small investment. The growth of your senior care business will depend on letting the public know that you are there, that you offer something of value, and that you will stand behind your products and services.

# MARKETING PLAN

A marketing plan is the key to the success of your business. It is a written document that details the necessary actions to achieve one or more marketing objectives. A marketing plan should be part of your overall business plan. A marketing plan contains a list of actions with a solid foundation.

**DEVELOPING A EFFECTIVE MARKETING PLAN**

1. Describe your company's unique selling proposition.
2. Define your target market.

    a. Effective marketing, planning and promotion will begin with current information about the marketplace. Talk to customers; study the advertising of other businesses in your community. Being interactive will help you assess your marketing strengths and weaknesses.

3. **Define your customers**

    a. Your current customer base- Elderly? Family member?

        i. Income, location, career level

    b. How your customers learned about your services

        i. Advertising, direct mail, internet, word of mouth, Yellow Pages...

c. Patterns or habits your customers and potential customers share

    i. Where they shop, what they read, watch, listen to.

d. Qualities your customers value most about your services

    i. Convenience, customer service, reliability, availability, affordability

e. Prospective customers – who are you not reaching?

Know your customers- their likes, dislikes, expectations. Since you will have limited resources target only those customers who are more likely to purchase your services. As your business grows and your customer base expands, then, you may need to consider modifying this section of the marketing plan to include other customers.

1. **Write down the benefits of you services and what they offer to your community.**

2. **Describe how you will position your services.**

3. **Define your marketing methods. Relationship, external, referral, gorilla, center of influence, advertising.**

## IDENTIFYING YOUR CLIENT

There are several groups that could easily be identified as your customer". This is not meant to be a comprehensive list, rather a good place to start.

First the obvious group is the senior population. This is being defined as individuals over the age of 70. As a general rule they may be suffering from mild disabilities such as arthritis or diabetes, or may have suffered a medical setback such as a broken bone or heart attack. This is the population most targeted by our "senior" competition. This group can often be reached by going to the senior health professionals that refer them for services.

In addition to the older senior there is the population of baby boomers. If your company is going to offer value added services this group may also benefit from the services provided by your company. Even if you only provide services to seniors, this population is most likely the family members ordering the services for their elderly parents. These are individuals approximately 45 to 65 who have expendable income and will be entering retirement in the next 20 years. This is a large segment of the population that is expected to affect buying and selling patterns as well as medical services. The approach to this group will focus more on **home** services then on **senior** services.

Senior clients are a little unique in that they are more likely to come through a referral from an agency that has already made contact with the client and is referring them on for additional services. This is defined as relationship marketing in the next section. Potential referrals may come from individuals or organizations such as:

- Area Agency on Aging (County Agency)—obtain their provider list
- Geriatrics Care Managers
- Senior Centers
- Skilled Nursing Facilities
- Assisted Living Centers
- Physician Office Centers (Internal and Geriatrics)
- Hospital Discharge Planners
- Physical and Occupational Therapists (Hospitals and Independent Facilities)—Will determine if grab bars are needed

# PROSPECT RESEARCH

For more general prospect research, you will find that area libraries are a resource that can be useful in narrowing the list of potential prospects down to the candidates who best fit the target profile. Libraries contain local newspapers with real estate sections, state and county service directories, business guides, and a number of other resources.

A few hours of work with the city telephone directory will also provide you with specific information. The directories are updated annually, and the large majority of businesses in most areas will be listed. The organization and listing formats vary somewhat from one locale to another. But most directories conform to the same organizational scheme: businesses are listed alphabetically by type. Depending on each community in your territory, you may have access to other business listings as resources for your research.

**Census Tracts and Zip Code Lists**
These listings state how many businesses are within a specific geographic area. Businesses are generally grouped into categories. This sort of information is very valuable in targeting your expansion market.

### Dun and Bradstreet Listings of Businesses

These lists are purchased by zip code and can be qualified by employee size.

### Local Government Offices

Your local city or county clerk will, in some jurisdictions, keep a listing of new businesses that have registered. Periodically check with your clerk's office for these new business listings.

Remember that conditions in your area are likely to be constantly changing as new residents and businesses move in and out. You will want to continually be on the lookout for new professionals, as well as changes in management and personnel.

Also, know and understand the benefits of your services so you will be prepared to answer questions. Remember, you are the expert. It is also helpful to take prospect leads lunch or some treat. This will help to break the ice.

## TYPES OF Advertising

### Relationship

This is one of the best forms of advertising that is available to you. It works effectively with business to business and professional to professional marketing. This method is used when long term relationships are crucial in securing leads from a referral source.

Relationship marketing is the most effective way to secure relationships in senior care and other senior related businesses. The cost associated with this marketing is small gifts of candy jars, donuts, etc as well as the time spent fostering these relationships. This type of marketing does not often see results overnight and should be a part of your long term marketing plan. Some examples of this marketing include; introduction letter, personal visits, cards, updates, e-mail and face to face networking with hospital case managers, home health, SNF and assisted living staff.

There are many examples of relationship marketing. As mentioned above this is the most common form of marketing in senior services.

**Health Fairs**

Attending health fairs can be beneficial. You should attend. Not only do these health fairs have great potential for providing you with quality leads, but they are also an excellent way for you to stay on top of industry developments and trends.

Many Senior Care Companies do not offer deep cleaning, handyman or yard care services. If you plan on providing any of these value added services these health fairs will give you a great opportunity market your services by making alliances with similar senior care businesses that do not offer value added services.

**Seminars/Speeches**

Simply by making speeches before large audiences, you will acquire an instant celebrity status. For the next one to four weeks after the speech, you will be able to use the "Hey, the guy/woman who did the speech is here to see us" effect to your business advantage. It is recommended that you speak about topics related to healthy elderly living in the home and provide numerous examples of products and services provided by your company. (Remember to always conclude your speeches with a "Thank You" and to extend to the assembled guests the invitation to download your presentation materials from your Web site

It is important that you focus on delivering speeches before groups that can provide referrals and enlist people for your services, including, but not limited to: decision makers from senior centers, skilled nursing facilities, assisted living centers, and physician office centers (internal and geriatrics). Moreover, you want to invite hospital discharge planners, case planners, and physical and occupational therapists.

## Business Alliances

Who around you is looking for the same customer? All else equal, people want to work with people they know, like and trust. Pass referrals to other organizations and ask them to do the same. Be a good partner. Pass more referrals than you receive. It will come back to you.

## Chambers of Commerce

Joining the chamber of commerce or other civic, business, or community organizations is an effective sales and promotional tool by expanding professional contacts. Becoming a prominent community member will assist with personal credibility when marketing within your community.

# External Advertising

This method, traditional defined as advertising, is a very effective tool in your businesses arsenal. This type of marking is the most expensive and results in the most immediate results. Your external marketing program should include the following tools;' door hangers, newspaper inserts, newspaper ads, internet marketing, and Coupon mailers. Direct mail is highly effective because you choose the zip code you target based on demographic studies. Radio and television may also be used. To be effective, this type of marketing needs to be performed consistently and repetitively to yield the best results. Do not make the mistake of judging effectiveness on the results of one advertisement. Studies show consumers need to see a company 5 to 7 times before they purchase services. In addition, this type of advertising must be more "direct response" advertising. There must be a coupon or some other "call to action" to yield results. Traditional, "institutional" advertising means putting your name out and trying to build your brand with no additional incentives and is not nearly as effective. Also, limit your offer to one service and sell additional services after you make contact with the client. Too many service offerings on one ad are confusing and less likely to cause the consumer to "act" on the ad.

External advertising requires the biggest financial investment and should be watched closely, tested and measured to assure your investment is as effective as possible. In placing any advertisement, consider the following:

## Size

The size of the ad, in relation to sizes of other ads and the format of the publication, can determine how well the ad will be seen and read.

## Position

The best position for an advertisement is "above the fold" (on the top half of a page) or towards the front of an issue. However, be wary of special placement costs. Remember, too, that a well laid out ad will attract attention wherever it is located.

## Color

Color is eye catching, but it can be expensive. Use caution when opting for special production techniques.

## Cost

Is the ad you have prepared too expensive? Some publications may be able to offer a package of repeat appearances at a discount so your ad will get more exposure. After placing your order, but before the ad appears in print, you should receive a proof of the ad. Check the accuracy of the following items on the proof:

- Phone number
- Address

- Any other copy

## Internet Marketing/Pay Per-Click Advertising/Leads

For the better part of a decade, pay-per-click has been the fastest growing advertising channel around. Unlike like other forms of advertising where it's impossible to figure out which part of your budget is most effective, with search marketing you can calculate the return on every ad you buy.

**But many successful advertisers report that their biggest challenge with PPC is that they can't buy enough traffic.**

Home Advisor (Formerly Service Magic) Home Advisor is a "pay for referral" business. Referrals cost between $10-15 per lead. Once you are notified, CALL IMMEDIATELY to set up the appointment.

Home Advisor is not the only lead generation/Pay for leads site out there. Care.com, Nations Carelink and many more work as well.

## Leads

A MIT behavioral study revealed when sales representatives had success around calling web-generated leads. To find these facts, we looked at leads that were captured through a web form, and attempted or called at least one time. Summarized below are some of the more interesting findings related to speed and timing when responding to web-generated leads:

- **Wednesdays** and **Thursdays** are the best days to **call** in order to contact (by **49.7%** over the worst day) and qualify (by **24.9%** over the worst day) leads. **Thursday** is the best day to contact a lead in order to qualify that lead (by **19.1%** better than the worst day).

- **4 to 6pm** is the best time to call to make **contact** with a lead (by **114%** over the worst time block). **8-9am** and **4-5pm** are the best times to call to **qualify** a lead (by **164%** better 1-2pm, the worst time of the day). **4-5pm** is the best time to contact a lead to **qualify** over 11-12am by **109%**).

- The odds of calling to contact a lead decrease by over **10 times** in the 1st hour. The odds of calling to **qualify** a lead decrease by over **6 times** in the 1st hour. After **20 hours** every additional dial your salespeople make actually hurts your ability to make contact to qualify a lead.

- The odds of contacting a lead if called in **5 minutes** versus **30 minutes** drop **100 times**. The odds of qualifying a lead if called in **5 minutes** versus **30 minutes** drop **21 times**.

Here is a link to the full study by MIT:

http://www.leadresponsemanagement.org/mit_study

In short, today's professional is making smarter decisions through social media.

Marketing tactics like e-mail and display advertising still work, but opportunities for deeper engagement through social media can help marketers build trust and relationships that ultimately yield a higher return on marketing investments.

**Yellow Pages** Such listing should be under the headings "Geriatric Care," "Elderly Care," "Maintenance Services/Care," "Yard Service/care," "Home Care," Personal Care," "House Keeping," or any other listings the you deem appropriate. In addition, you should maintain a boldfaced listing in the white pages of your local directory.

**Newspapers**

Newspaper advertising can provide useful exposure to , especially for messages that include specifically dated information (sale) or encourage a direct response (coupon).

However, one disadvantage of newspaper advertising is the over-exposure to people who may not be interested in, or who are unable to take advantage of, your services. Also, to reach target audiences in several communities, you may need to run the same ad in several newspapers, increasing your costs.

Before purchasing newspaper space, ask yourself:

- Who reads the paper? What are the ages, income, and educational levels of the readers? Do these characteristics correspond to those of your typical client?
- Is there a particular section of the paper that is more likely to be read by readers who could become new clients?
- How much will the ad cost? Can I get discount rates for repeat insertions?
- Is there a particular day the ad will work best?

**Magazines**

Niche magazine advertising is another option you might consider. This type of advertising provides you with the opportunity to promote your concept to an entire audience more likely to have an interest in your products and services.

Following are some magazine advertising issues you might consider:

- The ideal types of niche magazines for your ads are home-, family-, Geriatrics-, Physical Therapists-, and Occupational Therapists-oriented magazines.
- Magazines differ from newspapers in that they are published less frequently, have longer lead times from the date the advertising materials are due until the publication date (as long as two months), and have different advertising production requirements.
- Magazines sometimes offer advertisers special pricing for appearing in certain areas of the magazines, such as marketplace sections. This is a way for magazines to get advertisers with smaller budgets into their publications that might not otherwise be able to afford to advertise.
- Magazines will have special features each month that you might want to consider when making your advertising decisions. For example, a home magazine may have editorial content on Home Safety that will draw the best prospects. However, these special sections will also entice your competitors to advertise there as well, so readers might be inundated with advertising of products and services similar to those of your company.. It's a matter of testing to see which issues, etc., work best for you.

## CENTER OF INFLUENCE

This is marketing to and with the people you know. Family, friends and associates can all be customers and referrals. This type of marketing is very effective as you begin your business because your family and friends are often enthused about your new business venture and want to help. Sit down and think of as many people you know that would benefit from your services. Send all of these people an introductory letter offering your services with a "call to action." This is one of the least expensive methods of spreading the word of your business and can yield quick results. This is the type of marketing that can be done constantly thorough out the life of your business. Include in your list people such as; your physician, realtor, church friends, dentist and barista buddy.

## GORILLA MARKETING

This type of marketing is for those who have a limited budget and are looking for the most bang for your buck. A gorilla marketing campaign must be consistent to be effective. With gorilla marketing you are trying to reach as many people as possible using techniques that are outside the box. The most effective gorilla marketing program is a e-postcard campaign through the e-mail. I would recommend that you use I-Contact to set up and deliver your e-mails..

## Harvesting Email Addresses

Create your own opt-in newsletter email list. Send out your newsletter once a quarter to your current customers and those "did not close" prospects that you want to have as customers. The prospect's email address should be easy to get at the time of booking the estimate. How about sending them an email before your appointment and drive them to your web site or send out some collateral material in the form of an attachment.

The number one reason customers unsubscribe from emails is because the messages are not relevant to them. In order to remain pertinent, you have to know what your target audience wants.

## Social Media

An untapped (free) way to market your organization is through Social Media. People tend to work with people they know, like and trust. Become their trusted advisor. Send weekly tips through Twitter.com, Facebook and make sure to make your business connections through LinkedIn. In short, today's professional is making smarter decisions through social media.

Marketing tactics like e-mail and display advertising still work, but opportunities for deeper engagement through social media can help marketers build trust and relationships that ultimately yield a higher return on marketing investments.

**Referral Marketing**

This is the type of marketing you use after you have started getting customers. The idea is to give discounts to current customers for referring their friends and family. This is similar to the circle of influence only expanding into different circles. For referral marketing to be effective you must keep your clients happy. Health professionals, business people and executives usually have well-established networks of contacts to which they may refer you. It is quite likely that after your first few contracts, referrals will become a solid source of new leads. This is the most effective marketing because it results in nearly 100% success rate in your bids. This is also an inexpensive way to market.

Referrals can become your number one referral source if you go after it.

**Don't forget to position yourself:** "I am a referral based organization. I've grown my business through referrals and want you to know that the only way I get referrals is making sure you are 100% satisfied. Create t raving fans!

# PROSPECT MANAGEMENT

It is often said that most salespeople actively work only the top 20 percent of the leads on their lists; they plan to get around to the other 80 percent when they have time. Whatever the ratio, it is essential to the success of your sales effort that **all** leads with potential eventually be explored. The only way you can accomplish this is to have a prospect management system that enables you to know what is going on with your leads. Having a system helps you keep track of your prospects; you then have a history of the lead over a period of time. I suggest you use a contact management program such as Outlook or the ACT program in order to accomplish this task.

## Basic Filing

The following are six basic methods of filing records:

- Alphabetic

- Numeric

- Geographic

- Subject

- Chronological

- Tickler, or Day File

At the beginning of each month, you should go through the prospect follow-ups for that month.

## SELLING TO A PROSPECTIVE CLIENT

To maximize the use of your valuable time, it is very important that you identify the decision-maker in the target business or organization and make your presentation to that person. Giving presentations to people who do not have the authority to refer your company is a waste of your valuable time. Be sure you contact the right person.

To make prospects aware of your company and how it can truly benefit them, you must demonstrate to prospects that you really have something of value to offer. They may not immediately recognize the advantages of having your company. Take a moment and "wear the hat" of the person you are marketing to. What would make you purchase services? It is your responsibility to demonstrate the benefits of all your products and services.

## THE VALUE OF ADVERTISING

Advertising dollars, if well spent, offer a high rate of return for a small investment. The growth of your business will depend on letting the public know that you are there, that you offer something of value, and that you will stand behind your products and services. Advertising can promote specific specials or simply support the image and name of your business.

### Reach new clients.
Because conditions in your area are likely to be constantly changing as new residents move in and out, you will want to introduce yourself to all potential new clients.

### Meet the competition head on.
Your competitors may be employing newspaper, radio, and other effective advertising strategies. You must counter this exposure to hold on to your client base.

### Meet sales goals faster.
Regular advertising goes hand in hand with business growth. Relying on word of mouth alone to get your message to the public will unnecessarily slow the pace of your growth.

### Promote a positive Image In the community.
Maintain a healthy, positive image in the community by being visible through regular advertising.

**Promote employee enthusiasm.**

Regular advertising instills a sense of pride and mission in employees. Genuine employee enthusiasm translates directly to high-quality service and helps build repeat business from satisfied clients.

## THE BUSINESS/GRAND OPENING

The staging of a Business/Grand opening celebration can significantly promote the initial acceptance and success of your business. A Business opening will attract public attention, and it can build genuine enthusiasm among your staff and the community. Do not spend more than $1500 on a grand opening.

### Planning a business opening

The Business opening is your opportunity to introduce your services to the people in your community and for you to become acquainted with these potential clients. Because repeat business will be the lifeblood of your business, it is imperative that every client's interaction with you and your business is a pleasant one.

Plan and organize your Business opening activities well before the event so you present your business to the public in the best way possible.

**Business opening activities**

We recommend the following Business opening activities:

- Prepare a press release for distribution to the local business press that announces your opening and describes the products and services provided by your business.

- Print direct mail flyers/brochures with your business' name, address, telephone number, fax number, e-mail address, and your name.

- Order business letterhead stationery with all relevant business specific information.

- Order business cards with all relevant business specific information.

In addition, host an event (e.g., host a wine and cheese get together at a senior center or a Home Safety Fair, inviting discharge planners, therapists, case managers, etc.) to formally announce the opening of your business one month after you open. In preparation for this event, you should perform the following activities:

- Rent/Reserve space at a senior center or other appropriate venue.

- Mail formal invitations to your discharge planners,

case managers, physical therapists, occupational therapists, local businesses, family members, Chamber of Commerce, attorney, accountant, and close friends inviting them to attend your opening event.

- Present a keynote speaker to speak about topics of concern to your potential clients, (e.g., Safety in the Home). This speech should include a pitch for your products and services.

## ADDITIONAL ADVERTISING IDEAS

**Radio**

When considering the purchase of radio time on a particular station there are three items to keep in mind. First, think about the demographics of the listening audience (age, gender, geographical location, income, and educational background). Purchase radio time on a station that plays the kind of music to which the people of your area listen.

Second, repetition of an ad is an important factor in radio advertising. Many believe that frequent repetition during a limited period makes a lasting impression and is more easily recalled by listeners. According to this view, it is better to buy four spot announcements in one week than it is to buy four spot announcements over a period of a month.

A third consideration should be the time the radio spot runs. It may be beneficial to schedule spots during the time of day when your clients are most likely to be listening to the radio. However, prime air times also carry prime rates.

## Television

Television has undeniable impact on the viewing public. It is an emotional, active medium that has the potential of telling your story as no other medium can. Although television advertising is costly, local or cable television can be relatively affordable.

## Movie Theater Screen

Movie theater screen advertising is an incredibly cost-effective format that achieves tremendous reach. Depending on the theater chain, Screen Ads are either still or Digital; both command a captive audience, massive reach and tremendous recall!

## Still slides

Typically played within a pre-show entertainment program combining movie trivia, theater announcements and advertising slides, Still Slides display your message for approximately 13 seconds at an average of every 3 – 5 minutes. Each ad plays about 4 – 5 times prior to each feature presentation on every screen in the complex. To enhance the effectiveness of each ad, most theaters limit the number of advertisers allowed.

### Digital ads

Digital Slides transform a still slide into an engaging message with movement and sound. Much like a PowerPoint presentation on your computer, Digital Slides enhance your message with moving features like titles sliding across the screen, a phone number popping up, photos swooshing across the ad, etc. Your advertisement appears between 25 and 125 times per day, per theater complex.

## SPECIALTY ADVERTISING

Specialty advertising calls for the imprinting of your name, address, logo, slogan, etc., on items such as refrigerator magnets with calendars, notepads, pens, coffee mugs, caps, etc., to increase the visibility of your business' name. These items can be given to clients as free gifts when they contract for your services or as bonuses for purchases over a certain amount. Once referred to as "gimmick advertising," specialty advertising has attained a new level of professionalism: the quality of goods has improved and the public has demonstrated its interest in these items.

It is important to consider the audience you are trying to reach when looking at purchasing the items for your specialty-advertising program. Make an effort to choose only the novelties that will be the most appropriate and useful for your particular clients.

## PUBLICITY

Publicity, or "free" advertising, is the most economical way to promote your business. Consequently, it should be used whenever possible.

The opening of a business will be considered news in most communities. To notify the media of your opening, write a simple press release yourself. If you clearly state the facts (with very little puffery), the press release will usually be accepted, published and, in many cases, even welcomed in most area newspapers. However, because it may be used exactly as you have written it, you should make every effort to see that the information is accurate and free of grammar, spelling, and typing errors.

Local newspapers usually welcome information about new community developments as "fillers" for local newspaper business/finance sections. So do not hesitate to promote your enterprise through the use of press releases whenever it seems appropriats

SAMPLE PRESS RELEASE FORMAT

DATE

CONTACT PERSON

TITLE

PHONE NUMBER

RELEASE DATE

HEADLINE

DATE LINE (e.g., (CITY, STATE) (Insert copy here)

more - (if applicable) or # # #

## WORD-OF-MOUTH ADVERTISING

Do not forget that the best **free** advertising you can ever get is through your clients. Referrals are probably the most important way of generating new business.  If you provide quality products and services each and every time, your reputation will spread throughout the community in which you are located.

No amount of advertising, promotional materials, or free giveaways can ever compensate for poor services, bad products, or unprofessional behavior.  If you maintain high standards of excellence with your products and services, as well as integrity and cooperation, you will find that the free advertising you receive from your clients will be overwhelming with praise.  On the other hand, if you do not maintain high standards, you will find that this form of advertising can literally destroy your business.  So treat your best advertising resource—your clients—with great care.  Make sure your clients not only say good things about the products they received, but make sure they perceive real value from your products and services.

# COMMUNITY INVOLVEMENT

Maintaining a healthy, positive image in the community is another means of promoting your business. Your business is a local business, and good standing in the community can be an asset to you. Your active participation in the community can generate business for your concept.

As a businessperson, membership and participation in your local chamber of commerce is a beneficial form of civic involvement. This will promote good relations with neighboring businesses as well. Also, service organizations will provide you with exposure to other business professionals, help you become known in the community, enable you to learn valuable business lessons, and keep your name highly visible.

Communities offer a great deal of public relations opportunities. You are encouraged to become involved with community activities. Your business will become well known to neighboring communities through this involvement and will help you attract new clients.

Your goal is to make your name as prominent as possible and always in a positive light. Actively look for opportunities and take advantage of as many as possible.

Some ideas for possible community-service events include, but are not limited to:

- Sponsoring buses to take seniors on field trips and outings
- Hosting Health Fairs for the community

## FUNDING

When you put your marketing plan together you need to be willing and able to fund it properly to achieve your desired results. Just because you are spending money on marketing does not mean your marketing will be successful. You need to test and measure the results. You need to figure out the "break even" of your marketing campaign. One of the fastest ways to break your business is to ignore the breakeven point of your marketing campaign. If you're not making money on your marketing you shouldn't be doing it. You need to know your costs up front or you will have no idea what you need to achieve in order for the campaign to be worthwhile. If you determine the campaign has very little chance of success you need to go back to the drawing board. For example, if a TV commercial costs tens of thousands of dollars you will need to acquire several hundred clients from the ad. This may not be a realistic goal.

To work out the breakeven point you need to follow these steps; work out your total fixed costs. After you've worked out you're total fixed costs for the campaign, work out your profit (average dollar sales, minus your variable costs) this will allow you to determine how many responses you need in order to break even. Divide the number of responses you need by the total number of people your campaign will reach (anything over 5% for a direct mail is a stretch). Without knowing this figure, you can't know whether or not your advertising is working. If your campaign requires a 45% response rate you'll start going backwards at a rapid rate. It is also important to calculate this number so you can understand how much true profit you're making from each campaign. This allows you to compare one campaign to another. Since marketing is an investment, you need to be sure you are getting a good return on your money.

## Campaign Analysis

**Hard Costs**

Production     $_____

Paper          $_____

Printing $_____

Delivery $_____

Other $_____

1. **Total Fixed Cost** $_____
2. **Average $$ Sale** $_____

**Variable Costs**

Wages $_____

Electricity $_____

Telephone $_____

Rent $_____

Brochures $_____

Other $_____

3. **Total Variable** $_____

**Delivery Cost**

Cost of Goods Sold $_____

Taxes $_____

Transportation $_____

Packaging     $_____

Other         $_____

4.  **Total Delivery**     $_____


5.  **Net Profit [2/(3+4)]**      $_____


6.  **Response to Break Even (1/5)** $_____

## CLOSING THOUGHTS

Advertising keeps your services in the public's eye by creating a sense of awareness. Yet this awareness alone will not ensure the success of your business. Thus, advertising not only has to be effective, it also has to be a continuous process.

Remember:

- In order to get someone to buy, we need to touch him or her on an average of **seven** times before they buy.
- Make sure you publish your email address and web address on everything you publish online or in print.
- Track, to the best of your ability, to know where your inquiries are coming from. Track your inquiries, appointments and closes. Know what your close rates are!

You are going to lose customers in this business. You will sometimes not meet the client's expectations. Some of your customers will move, get divorced, some will pass on or they might lose their job and can't afford you anymore.

Tips:

- A good benchmark to shoot for is keeping your permanent cancellation rate below 2.5%. This is based on 100.
- A good benchmark is a temporary cancel rate of less than 4%. This is also based on 100. This number is usually indicative of your customer services levels.
- A good profit margin is anything above 25%.
- For recurring services evaluate your working rate on a regular basis. If we have a number of clients falling well below our actual hourly rate the estimator(s) are "under pricing." Adjustments will need to be made in the future with a price increase letter after 8-10 services completed.
- Always give the customer the benefit of any doubts until they prove to you otherwise.

# CHAPTER 5

# HANDS ON MARKETING

## Marketing to Senior Housing

## Assisted Living, Independent Living, & Skilled Nursing Facilities

### Definitions:

**Independent Living:** Communities are often designed as private campuses. Many feature pools, spas, exercise centers, & social halls. Meal plans are organized, some offer varying forms of health care; but often, residents are accountable for their own well being.

**Assisted Living:** Assisted livings are a type of long-term community for elderly or disabled people who are able to get around on their own with minor assistance. However, they may need help with some activities of daily living, having their meals in a central dining area, activities, and having nursing staff on call.

**Skilled Nursing:** Skilled Nursing Facilities offer 24 hour nursing care, rehabilitation services such as physical, speech, & occupation therapy; assistance with personal care, assistance with personal care activities such as eating, walking, toileting, and bathing; coordinated management of patient care; social services; and activities.

## Setting the Appointment

1. Research the company that you will be contacting...websites, phonebook ads, senior resource guides, and area agency on aging...know the services they provide. You could do some research by being a "Secret Shopper" by posing as a family member wanting information about the community.

2. Phone ahead to schedule a face to face appointment to meet with the Marketing/ Sales Director.

3. When calling, here are some tips :

   "I am new to this area/industry and would like to learn more about your company and the services you provide"

   "I will be in your area on Wed & Thurs, would it be ok to stop by and meet with your for a few minutes?"

   "I have heard great things about your community; I'd like to learn more"

   "I am trying to learn about the resources available to seniors, when we can no longer serve our clients at home; we want to know how to refer to you"

4. Be sure to let them know you realize that they are very busy and ask them if they could spare a few minutes with you.

5. If the Marketing Director says that they don't have time, ask if there is a better time to call for an appointment, or if they are very resistant, ask if it would be ok to drop off information for them as a last resort.

6. If the Marketing Director agrees to set up a time, let them know that you have a short commercial/presentation about our company that is very unique to this industry.

7. Try not to give your commercial over the phone; it's hard to build relationships over the phone.

8. Try to let them know that you are not pushy salesmen; make it about them, learning about their services.

9. You will want to research the licensing for the Assisted Living and Independent Living Communities. Some states have certain regulations. Find out how much care they can provide to their residents. ???

10. Some communities have specific days set aside to meet with vendors/providers.

## The Appointment

- Call the day before your appointment to confirm the time and make sure that it still is ok with them.

- Day of the Appointment: Show up ON TIME.

- Dress Professional, wear close toed shoes, and a nametag, remember that you are an invited guest in their resident's home.

- Check in with the Receptionist/Concierge, let them know that you have an appointment with "Jon Brown"...they may have a visitor sign in sheet that you will need to sign in. (Some communities are very particular about that with visitors) The Receptionists are the gate keepers, be sure to remember their name, develop a relationship with them...when dropping off treats or information, be sure to give them a treat also.

- When meeting with the marketing director, try to meet in a quiet place, the lobby tends to be very noisy and in personable, you want their undivided attention.  Try not to have your information out, bring your information in a bag/briefcase, not to look like an overwhelming salesman.
- Tips to say when meeting starts:
- "Thank you so much for taking the time to meet with me, I know that you are very busy".
- "Tell me a little about your background, how did you get started in this industry?"
- "How long have you been with the company?"
- What you want to do is put them at ease and not push your services up front.  You will want to learn about their company and find out what you think you can offer them to help them be successful with their census/occupancy.  Keep in mind, their number one goal is to fill the building!
- The first thing you want to do is build a rapport with that person. Let them lead the conversation...find out everything out about them.
- As they are explaining to you what services they provide, listen carefully...what are their goals?
- Once you have learned about their services, now you can tailor your presentation to them.

- First, tell them a little about yourself, why you started your business, then lead in to your presentation.
- If you have a laptop proceed with the PowerPoint presentation or flip chart, ask if it would be ok to show them the presentation.

**Presentations to Independent/Assisted Living Communities**

When presenting, keep in mind that their number one goal is to fill their building & keep it full.  There will be times when one of their residents is having a difficult time, maybe from an illness, or recuperation from a hospitalization...that would be a good time to educate them about our personal care/companionship services.  Emphasize to them you understand how important it is for the resident to remain in their home-like environment, which they will agree with you.  Explain to them that you can offer short periods of respite care, or long term services so they can remain in their community without interruption. Let them know that you are professional in appearance, and have extensive training.

Another service you can offer to these communities is relocation services.  If you choose to provide relocation services as an added value proposition to these communities it can help you stand out above the competition.

How you can approach this, is educating them about how you can work hand in hand with their move-ins.  Some markets are very competitive and are looking for a way to stand out by offering something different, setting them apart from the others.  They appreciate the value of relocation services because the biggest obstacle is gathering all of the family members to help with the move, sometimes they need to wait for them to come into town, can only move mom in on a Saturday, ...delaying their move-in.

Chances are that the community prefers the resident to move in during the week, there are more staff members to be of support at that time. By offering the move-in services, the communities don't lose income on an empty apartment. Some communities have a move-in offer...they will pay $250 - 300 towards their moving experiences. How it works with a local retirement community, you submit the total bill to the community; they credit the family $300 & bill them for the remainder.

There are many ways you can work with these communities. If they are not willing to offer that as a move-in incentive, then ask them to include your brochure with their move-in packets.

Explain to them the value of having your company do their move. You are senior friendly, will be careful with the furniture, making sure to not damage their walls, doors, etc. Find out when the elevators are available, being sure not to tie up the elevators at meal times, which entrance would be suitable for the movers to use, etc. A big challenge for a new move-in is that once the items are delivered, the staff doesn't have a lot of time to unpack the resident, hang pictures, dispose of the boxes, & put things away. The goal of the community is to make their first day an enjoyable experience for both the resident & family. Your job is to help the community look good!

If the community has more than one senior product, they might have an Alzheimer's unit, or Skilled Nursing Unit. If the resident needs a different level of care, let them know that you can do in-house moves.

Another thing you want to remember is that their residents move out also, you are just as good moving-in as you are moving them out. If a death occurs, sometimes it is very difficult for the family to pack their loved-ones belongings and move them out, you are very sensitive to those issues.

Another approach is offering your handyman services. If you are going to offer handyman services as a continual value added service, I would recommend that you hire a full time handyman. If you are going to offer handyman services on an as needed basis then I would recommend you find a qualified handyman to contract these services to.

Assisted Livings will sometimes need your handyman services. An example would be if the Assisted living Facility had a surge of discharges at one time, leaving many apartments that needed to be painted, cleaned, turned around, & rent-ready...overwhelming their maintenance department. Be aware that some Maintenance Directors might be defensive, (Territorial) and not be open to that idea. Emphasize that you can have a symbiotic relationship, we work with clients that may eventually need their services, it can work both ways.

If they have time, it would be a great idea to tour their community; it is an opportunity to meet other department managers along the way.

A goal of yours will be to set up a time to present your power point to the managers...maybe offer to bring in donuts one morning after one of their meetings?

## Presentations to Skilled Nursing Facilities/Rehab Centers

As you are meeting with Skilled Nursing Facilities, you will have a different approach; you want to meet with the Marketing Director & Discharge Planners/Case Managers.

When meeting with the marketing director, you will want to show the power-point presentation to introduce Your Company.  They meet with a lot of families and are in a position to refer to our services on a regular basis.  If a client is not ready to move-in to a center, they might benefit from our personal care services.  The goal would be to present to their department managers.

When meeting with the Discharge/Care Managers, they arrange for all of the services at time of discharge from their rehab stay.  They might discharge to home, Assisted Living, or an Independent Living Community.  If your company offers handyman services, they will appreciate the fact that you can install grab bars & wheel chair ramps to help their clients stay safe.  The goal for this visit is to present to their rehab staff and let them know that we work hand in hand with the Home Health agencies.

A lot of times the facilities will host events and are always looking for co-sponsors for them, ask them if you can participate in one of those events…it will get your name out to those patients who will be returning home. If time allows, ask if you may tour their facility.

If you are unable to meet with the Sales/Marketing Directors, drop off information in an envelope with their name on it. Sometimes receptionists throw away brochures and never make it to the Marketing Directors. Follow up with a phone call to make sure they received the information and see if you can set up an appointment to meet with them.

The goal is to take your presentation to the next step, who else would benefit from your Services?

When meeting with the Marketing Directors, ask them about senior organizations that they belong to, and any networking opportunities. Ask if you could tag along and be their guest when attending the meetings. It is a lot easier to meet other professionals when being introduced by another senior care provider. They tend to have a lot of connections and resources.

If your budget allows, give them your brochures and a pen, mug, or something that they will hold on to. Try not to give them too many brochures; it gives you an opportunity to drop off more at a later time….always find a chance to visit them. Before you leave, ask them if it would be ok to drop by maybe weekly, or bi-weekly to stop in to say hello, or if it would be more appropriate to make appointments with them in the future. After meeting with them, write them a thank you note.

There are opportunities to participate in associations...for Assisted Living; each state will have an Assisted Living Association, Each state will have a State Health Care Association, & some states will have an association for Independent Living.  They have yearly conferences & have opportunities for vendors to participate in their conferences.  This will give you good exposure to the attendees.

## Marketing to Home Health/Hospice Agencies

**Definitions**:

**Home Health Agency**:  Home Health Agencies brings skilled nursing and other services on an **intermittent**, visiting basis into the client's home, treatment, cure or relief of a health condition, illness, injury or disease.

**Hospice Agencies**:  Hospice Agencies means a licensed program providing care and support to terminally ill clients and their families.

**Home Health/Hospice Agencies** are sometimes sensitive to the fact that you provide home services, thinking that you are their competition, but in fact you work hand in hand with them.   When their client no longer requires skilled services that is where your company can step in and provide the personal care for their clients.

**Setting the appointment**

- Research the company you will be contacting...websites, phonebook ads, senior resource guides, and area agency on aging....know the services they provide.  You could do some research by being a "Secret Shopper" by posing as a family member wanting information about the community.

- Phone ahead to schedule a face to face appointment.
- When calling, here are some tips:

"I am new to this area/industry and would like to learn more about your company and the services you provide".

"I will be in your area on Wed & Thurs, would it be ok to stop by and meet with you for a few minutes"?

"I have heard great things about your agency; I'd like to learn more".

There are a few avenues to approach these companies...I have found that the Marketing Directors/Community Liaisons are probably your best bet to setting up a presentation. Try to meet with the marketer first to educate them about your company.

HH & Hospice Agencies have certain requirements for providing continuing in-services & training for their staff. A good time to present to them is right before or after their in-services, that way you will have all of the staff there. The Marketing Directors can direct you to who you need to contact to set up a presentation...generally it is the Director of Nursing. I have found that if you take food into them, they will be more willing to set up the presentation.

You can start out a conversation with the Marketing Directors by asking them to tell you about their agency, get a feel for the services they provide. Let them you know that you are looking to partner with a few local agencies to refer to when your clients need skilled care at home. The goal for this marketing call is to be invited to do a presentation to their key staff, i.e.: Director of Nursing, Social Workers, Nurse Case Managers, Rehab, and CNA's.

**The Presentation**

Call the day before to confirm the appointment. Show up on time. Have with you brochures, give-a-ways, & your lap top. If it is a big crowd, you will want to present with an LCD projector.

Introduce yourself and let them know your story, why you opened your company. At that time, you can ask to go around the room and have them tell you their name and position, so you will know who the key players in the company are.

Once introductions are over, proceed to the presentation. Some key points you will want to discuss is that you are not competition; you work hand in hand with them.

Suggestions: "When you client is discharged to home from a hospital or rehab facility, educate them about any of your value added services, such as handyman, cleaning, yard services, 24 hour care, etc. Their goal is to help their clients stay home in a safe environment.

If they have a client who is on Home Care/Hospice educate them about our housekeeping services. Emphasize the necessity of having the home clean to prevent infection and focus on healthy living. For Hospice clients, their agency can't be by their side all of the time. Offer them our personal care services.

Home Health & Hospice agencies can be your best referral source; they look for companies to partner with to provide non-skilled services to their clients. Ask them if they belong to any senior associations, if they do, can you tag along with them to meet their colleagues?

Ask if there is a state association for Home Health/Hospice? They generally have yearly conferences and will have opportunities for vendors. This will give you great exposure to the attendees.

**Follow-up**

Send them a thank you note. Keep in touch with your key players. Ask them if it is ok to stop in to replenish brochures & keep in touch. The key is follow-up!

# Marketing to Hospital Case Managers/Discharge Planners & Doctors

Marketing to hospitals & Doctors will vary from city to city. It is a very delicate market. Some hospitals will be open to your presentations, some will not. They are overloaded from vendors trying to sell them their services.

### Setting the Appointment with Hospitals

In most cases, the Case Managers have a main office. There will be a receptionist/gate keeper. Do not attempt to contact the case managers directly, go through the proper channels. When talking with the gate keeper, be very aware that they are being inundated with Home Health/Hospice Agencies, Skilled Nursing Facilities, Assisted Living

Communities, etc.

Ask for a date to do a presentation/in-service, ask if you can bring lunch, or a snack? Some Hospitals are very picky about bringing food/give-a-ways. Most of the time, you can only bring brochures. They usually schedule out months in advance. Be sure to build a relationship with the gate keeper.

**The Presentation**

Call a week ahead of time to confirm the appointment, or go in and speak with the gate keeper to confirm...you might want to ask the gate keeper if they would like a reminder brochure to put in the case manager's boxes. You can make up a flyer, letting them know about the presentation you have scheduled, letting them know you are looking forward to meeting them.

Arrive on-time; find out ahead of time to see if you should use an LCD projector or just use the lap-top to do the presentation. Have your brochures with you, and especially pricing info. They will want to know the costs.

Start out with introducing yourself, ask for them to introduce themselves and which area of the hospital they work in. i.e.: Rehab, Orthopedics, Medical Floor, & Oncology...are they Social Workers? Case Managers...who does the discharge planning?

While you are presenting your information, keep in mind that they are the first point of contact with families when planning to discharge to home, nursing facility, or a rehab facility. Many times the families are in a crisis and rely on the social workers/case managers for guidance.

At this time, families usually disclose their financial information, to see if they are eligible for county or state assistance. If you are contracted with these Government Programs, let them know that you provide services for these programs. Case Managers like to hear that you will help make their job easier. When case managers call with a referral, you want to respond very quickly. Their job is to discharge patients in a timely manner, some will have only hours to arrange for services. Some will want you to meet with the patient before discharge, some will not.

Find out what the procedure is if you are called in to meet with the patient. Hospitals will sometimes have you check in with the case management office, & wear a vendor badge, some won't be as stringent. The Hospitals don't like you on the floor without identifying yourself, or getting prior authorization. They are very concerned with HIPPA compliance.

Send each case manager a thank you card/gift.

**Follow-up**

Ask how they would like you to follow up with them...how often? Ask if you can replenish your brochures, drop off goodies? Do they allow goodies?

**Setting the Appointment with Doctors Offices**

Before calling, do some researches...check their specialties, and which hospitals they are affiliated with?  Do I know the doctors of my current clients? That would be an excellent start...to let them know you are caring for their patient and give him/her an update on their progress.

Doctors to target...General Practice, Internists, Orthopedics, OB/GYN, Geriatric, Neurologists, and the list could go on and on.  Target a few to start out.

Go in to the Doctor's office and introduce yourself to the receptionist, ask if you can speak with the office manager or the person who sets up in-services/luncheons.  Remember that they are being bombarded with Drug Reps, Home Health/Hospice Agencies, and Skilled Nursing Facilities.  When you speak with the person who schedules the appointments, introduce yourself, let them know that you understand that they are very busy, ask if lunch or breakfast would be better?  They might be scheduled out months in advance, get on their schedule and ask to be contacted if there is a cancellation.  Most offices are more accommodating when a meal is provided.

The Doctor Offices' goal is to help their patient be safe and well cared for.  The doctors are not usually the one who do the referring...it is their nurses.  They are the ones who are in contact the most and receive the multiple phone calls from the patient and their families.

**Presentation**

Go in to the office to confirm the appointment a week before to get a final count for the numbers of meals, snacks to provide...always ask if their employees are vegetarians or on low-carb diets.  Doctor's offices are tricky, most times they do not take their lunch break at the same time, you may have a few straggle in at a time. You might want to have your lap top with the slide that lists our services. You might be telling your story 10 times that day. Be sure to meet with the Doctor's nurses... they will have the most contact with the families. Use the power point presentation that was sent to you for Home Health/Hospice Agencies.

# Marketing to Guardians, Conservators, Geriatric Case Managers, Durable Medical Equipment (DME) Companies, & Senior Centers

### Definitions:

**Guardian:** A guardian is a person appointed by the court to protect the legal rights of another person called the Protected Person. If the court decides the protected person is incapacitated or incapable of taking care of him or her, it may give the guardian authority to make all decisions regarding **healthcare...personal & living care.**

Conservator: A conservator is a person appointed by the court to take care of the property or estate of another person who is considered by the court to be unable of handling their own **financial** affairs. The conservator is responsible to the court for how the Ward's funds or property are managed.

**Geriatric Case Manager:** Professional Geriatric Care Managers are health and human services specialists who help families care for older relatives, while encouraging as much independence as possible. The PGCM may be trained in any of a number of fields related to long-term care, including, but not limited to, nursing, gerontology, social work, or psychology, with a specialized focus on issues related to aging and elder care.

The PGCM acts as a guide and advocate – identifying problems and offering solutions.

Durable Medical Equipment Companies (DME): Durable equipment includes hospital beds, wheelchairs, canes, and walkers may be furnished on a rental basis or purchased.

Senior Centers: Senior Centers are designed to provide a social atmosphere, learning environment & lunch for seniors provided by County Aging Services.

**Setting the Appointment**

Research the company that you will be contacting...websites, phonebook ads, senior resource guides, and area agency on aging...know the services they provide.

It is important to phone ahead to schedule a face to face appointment to meet with them.

When calling, here are some tips:

"I am new to this area/industry and would like to learn more about your company and the services you provide".

"I will be in your area on Wed & Thurs, would it be ok to stop by and meet with you for a few minutes"?

"I am trying to learn about the resources available to seniors".

Be sure to let them know you realize that they are very busy and ask them if they could spare a few minutes with you. If they say they don't have time, ask if there is a better time to call for an appointment, or if they are very resistant, ask if it would be ok to drop off information for them as a last resort.

**The Appointment**

Call the day before your appointment to confirm the time and make sure that it is still ok with them.

Day of the appointment: Show up ON TIME...have your brochures and be sure to include price lists. The Conservators will want to know pricing. When meeting with them, try to meet in a quiet place, the lobby tends to be very noisy.

When you are first meeting with these professionals, find out all about their services, who their target audience is before you educate them about your company. As you are listening to them, find out their needs, how can your company help make them successful?

Tell them a little about yourself, why you started your company.

Proceed to the power point presentation.

**A few notes about each target audience**

Some Guardians/Conservators are employed by the state, or they may have their own private practice. They are especially careful when managing their client's needs; they look for the most cost effective services to offer to them. They will appreciate a price list.

Geriatric Care Managers are a great referral source...they work with both the clients and their family members...usually when a care manager is involved, there are usually some family dynamics that go along with their cases. Try to stay out of the families' situation; you are there to serve the client and the Care Manager. The Care Manager is usually the one who hire you and reimburse you directly.

Durable Medical Equipment Companies are a great referral source...they work with both seniors and their children. Grab bars and adaptive equipment is sold at these businesses and they will need a company to refer to for the installation. If they are already providing equipment to their customers; they know their health situation while they are in their homes servicing their equipment. The goal for this type of company is to give a presentation to the entire staff...from their service techs to sales staff.

Senior Centers are different in each county. Some centers are looking for volunteers to help serve their daily meals; some don't due to health & safety codes. The directors of the centers are very familiar with the members of the center and know their current living situations and are in a great position to refer them to your company. There are many ways you can partner with the centers...they are always looking for volunteers to teach a class or help with an event such as a dance. Most centers allow companies to sponsor refreshments for an event. Legally they cannot ask you to sponsor, you will have to offer your assistance. These events allow you to visit with the seniors, hand out information, and give away door prizes.

## Marketing to Senior Professionals, Attorneys, Trust Officers, Reverse Mortgage Brokers, & Non-profit Agencies

Each of these different areas of senior services, they all have one thing in common; they work directly with seniors and are in a position to refer to your company.

Senior professionals may consist of:

Certified Senior Care Managers, Religious affiliations, DME (Durable Medical Equipment) companies, Counselors, Educators Financial Counselors, Guardians, Conservators, and Support Group Leaders

## Marketing to Attorneys, Trust Officers, & Non-Profit Agencies

### A few notes on these target audiences

**Elder Law Attorney:** These attorneys are a great referral source...they meet with seniors and their family members. They are aware of funding sources and how to qualify for them.

**Trust Officers:** Trust Officers are usually involved when there is a large sum of money being managed for a senior. They are always looking for affordable choices for services and help their customers save money.

**Non-Profit Agencies:** These agencies are always looking for volunteers and partnership/financial opportunities. Align yourself with an agency who works with a lot of seniors...such as The Alzheimer's Association, American Diabetes Association, and The Arthritis Foundation. Most of these agencies hold fundraising events, such as walks and galas, at these galas; most of them have silent auctions and are looking for donations for them. This is a great time to donate your services, to get your name out...maybe a gift certificate for 3 hours of housekeeping services.

### Setting the appointment

Before calling these professionals, do some research; find out who their clientele is. Look them up on the internet, in your senior directories, and ask other healthcare professionals about them.

When calling, let them know that you are new to the area, wanting to know about the services they provide to seniors.

### The Appointment/Presentation

Follow the same procedure as the previous trainings for Marketing to Senior Housing and Home Health/Hospice agencies. Find opportunities to do a presentation to their co-workers.

### Follow-up

Be sure to keep in touch with your referral sources. Ask them how often you can call on them and find opportunities to keep in touch with them.

**Marketing Note**

As you are marketing to these professionals, you may not get immediate referrals, but they are in contact with a lot of other professionals and their clients. You want your company to be fresh on their mind. Ask if they belong to various associations, find out if you can join them, or be a sponsor at one of their meetings or conferences.

# Referrals

You know you are doing something right when you start getting referrals from your existing clients. If you don't ask for referrals, you won't get them.

A very subtle way to ask for referrals is by having your team leave a card behind from you to your client thanking them for their business and asking them, "Do you know someone who this service could help?" How powerful is the opportunity to leave the client a handwritten note on their kitchen counter. What are the chances of this getting read? You may want to offer a referral fee with a referral.

Referrals can be even more effective than merge mail as a lead source. It could become your number two referral source if you go after it.

# Company Marked Vehicles

What you will find out over time that if you have company marked vehicles driving around your territory, they are the *number one* lead source. The vehicle is a "rolling billboard." Obviously you cannot offer all of your employee's company vehicles; however you may offer a "stipend" for gas if they put magnetic signs on their own vehicles during work hours.

## Pricing

Consider the cost of your employee pool when determining pricing. Do not be tricked into playing the pricing game. You offer more services and better trained staff. You are not going to be the least expensive provider in the market. Quality cost money. Please see employee pay structure.

## Payment

Offer two types of payment for service: credit card or check. Do **not** offer billing or invoicing as an option! Stay away from cash if at all possible unless you are receiving it yourself.

Lay down the ground rules now. You will have payroll to cover, you need your money now. Do not create an accounts-receivable nightmare for yourself. Do you want to be sending out invoices on Saturday morning?

About 40% of your clients should sign up for the auto bill to their credit card thereby racking up frequent flyer miles or rebates. Write down all of their credit card information including the card verification number on the back. You might want to write this down on something other than the estimate form.

# CHAPTER 6

# VALUE ADDED SERVICES

## SENIOR RELOCATION SERVICES

### Question to Ask Client Prior to Move

1. Date/Time/Location of move. Fill out client information sheet.
2. Would you like us to assist you in packing your belongings?
3. Would you like us to assist you in unpacking your belongings at your new residence?
4. Where are you moving to? (Assisted living, family member's home, etc.)
5. What major appliances are you taking with you?
6. Do you have any items that will need special consideration? (Pianos, large pictures, large mirrors, antiques, etc.)
7. Would you like us to clean your old residence after the move?
8. Would you like us to clean your new residence prior to the move?

## Items Client Should Take Care of Prior to Move

(or arrange for us to take care of prior to move)

1. Reserve the elevator for moving (if applicable)
2. Reserve a moving time at assisted living center (if applicable)
3. Defrost refrigerator and freezer
    a. This should be done the day before and the doors should be left open for several hours before the move to prevent water spillage.
4. Gas line for gas dryer should be disconnected and capped off by a professional technician.
5. Drain fuel from any power tools that will be transported.

## MOVER SAFETY

1. Wear protective footwear with slip resistant soles.
2. Know where to put down a load before you lift it.
3. Never hurry when carrying a load. Take time if the load is heavy; set it down and rest periodically. Your strength will last longer with occasional rests.
4. Keep children and pets out of moving area.
5. Lift boxes and items properly
    o Proper Lifting Procedure
        ▪ Stand with feet shoulder width apart.

- Bend at knees, not at waist; keep your trunk vertical.
- Use both hands and slowly stand up. Don't twist torso.
- Hold item as close to body as possible to prevent back stress.
- Set the item down the same way you picked it up.

## PACKING TIPS

### Packing Materials

To make your move as efficient and organized as possible, you should obtain the following materials:

1. Boxes
2. Packing tape
3. Packing paper & peanuts
4. Bubble wrap
5. Moving pads
6. Dolly
7. Furniture movers (if available)
8. Plastic wrap

### Packing Table

Set up a worktable or cover the kitchen or dining room table so that you can do the majority of your packing on it in the upright position. Bending and stooping to pack will wear you out quickly and cause muscle aches. Keep this work area as open as possible to make the packing task easier for you. Keep all your packing materials at this table so you don't have to spend time searching for needed materials.

**Taping Boxes**

Tape reinforces the strength of the box which helps prevent damage. It is best to use three strips of tape on the bottom of a box. Make sure the tape reaches halfway up the box on both sides. Use another two or three strips of tape on the top. Never leave any boxes open. Open boxes are difficult to stack and lead to damage.

**Packing Boxes**

Try to use boxes that are the same size so you can best utilize the space within the moving truck. When packing a box place heavier items toward the bottom and lighter items on top. For your own benefit don't exceed 50 lbs. per box. Fill all extra space within the box with packing materials. Bunched up packing paper is the best. Packing peanuts can be hard to handle and move around easily. Bubble wrap can lose its cushioning if some of the bubbles pop. Try to avoid using newspaper as well. Newspaper print residue must be hand washed off of all things it touches;

dishwasher washing will not take it off. Also, print residue can ruin porous items like clay pots or lampshades or items with a rough finish like computer equipment.

**Glassware and other Fragile Items**

Thoroughly wrap items with enough paper so they do not clatter within the box. Use plenty of paper to line the top and bottom of each box. Glasses should be wrapped individually and placed standing up. Mark and place all fragile boxes together.

**Marking Boxes**

Mark the top and sides of all cartons by writing on the tape after the box is sealed shut. Describe contents and destination location (such as bedroom, kitchen, or basement). Have the writing on the box facing up to indicate which side of the box is up and which is down so that your movers don't turn the box upside down during moving.

Marking boxes well will make identifying where things are in them easier when they are stacked on top of each other or in their new location. If the box is being reused, then using fresh tape over marked tape eliminates old markings. Some packers like to use color-coding such as colored tape wrapped once around the box or colored stickers pasted on the box to identify in what room at the destination to put the box.

A client may ask you to keep inventory of all packed items. If this is to be done don't set your inventory list down anywhere but the packing table so you know where it is at all times.

## Furniture

Furniture items such as dressers, tables, bookcases, etc. should be wrapped with blankets or pads for protection. Blankets and pads should not be removed until the item is in new place at the new residence. Wrap items on top, all four sides, and bottom if necessary to ensure full protection. Dressers, desks, and other furniture with drawers should be wrapped in plastic wrap so they drawers don't fall out. If disassembly of furniture is required, place all screws and other hardware in a plastic bag and attach bag to furniture with furniture safe tape

## Elderly Clients or those with Alzheimer's

Sometimes clients may need items placed in their new residence just as they've been at their original home to ease the stress of moving. One easy way to do this is to wrap certain furniture pieces with plastic wrap while keeping everything inside. Use this procedure for items such as dressers, file cabinets, night stands, etc.

Clothes should be taken out of the closet in order and placed back at their new residence in the same way.

**Unwanted Items**

As you are packing and loading the home owner may want to discard unused/unwanted items to simplify their move. Make a designated area for these items that is out of the way. Wait until everything is packed and loaded in the truck before you take these items to the dump; you will most likely be adding to this pile all day. If there are only a few items see if using the street trashcan is an option, thus saving you a trip to the dump.

Be aware of and follow your state disposal rules. (Paint, TVs, Computers, Oil, Toxic Items).

## LOADING THE TRUCK

**Item Placement**

1. Move and load the heaviest items in the truck first. This included major appliances, large furniture, and other items that take more than two people to move. Place these

items at the far end of the truck, closest to the cab in the upright position. Place heavy items on either side to balance out the weight of the truck. Use pads and blankets to protect wood surfaces and corners.

2. Move longer such as mattresses, headboards, mirrors, and table tops in next. Place these items against the longest wall and upright to save space.

3. Load heaviest and largest boxes next. Places boxes on appliances and furniture. Fill up any available spaces such as under desks, chairs, etc.

4. Move in the lighter boxes next place on top of heavier boxes. Always make sure the lightest boxes are on top.

5. Load fragile and awkward items in last. Ensure that they will not move about during the trip.

**Loading Tips**

1. The truck should be large enough to accommodate 10-15% more of what you own. Too much room is better than too little room.

2. Use a dolly that has straps and are the right size. Pull the dolly up the ramp backwards and have someone follow behind to make sure nothing slips. Don't over load the dolly. It's better to make more trips than risk your safety.

3. When moving bicycles make sure to remove the front wheel. This ensures the bike will not move around during transport.

## MOVING IN

### Be Careful

After packing up and loading a truck you will be tired. Don't rush the move-in. Make sure you have good holds on items and take rests periodically. Most nicks and dings happen during the move in. Watch out for door frames, door handles, corners, and railings.

If moving into an assisted living center keep an eye out for residents. They will be curious who is moving in and want to see what is happening. Residents always have the right-of-way. Pause at doorways, entrances, and hallways if a resident is trying to pass. Remember to follow the safety tips.

### Organization

If you have followed the aforementioned moving procedures staying organized while unloading should be relatively simple. Take the boxes you marked previously to their designated rooms.

If helping those who will have a hard time with change, place furniture and items in same way as it was at the previous residence. This is especially important with bedroom and bathroom items.

Break down boxes as you unpack to give you more room and eliminate clutter.

## CLEANING SERVICES

In this section I am going to give you a quick tutorial on how to run the cleaning operations as part of your value added services in your senior care company. If you would like a more in depth book on how to run a profitable cleaning company please purchase my book titled "**Clean Up in the Cleaning Business**." It is available for purchase on Amazon.com.

### Scheduling

Everyone wants their homes cleaned on Thursday and Friday - it isn't possible. The Monday, Tuesday, Wednesday cleaning slots are tougher to fill. You might adjust your prices down a couple of bucks to fill these slots up.

Let me explain: A typical residential cleaning companies' teams and routes need to be optimized to make any money for the owners or the cleaning teams. The same is true for your senior care company. Optimal route utilization for a cleaning team of two would be four properties a day, five days a week, or 20 regular cleans per team per week. Many teams don't want to work that hard so cleaning 13-17 homes a week is okay for them.

## Payment

Offer two types of payment for service: credit card or check.

Do not offer billing or invoicing as an option! Stay away from cash if at all possible. Cash disappears.

Lay down the ground rules now. You will have payroll to cover, you need your money now. Do not create an accounts-receivable nightmare for yourself. Do you want to be sending out invoices on Saturday morning?

About 40% of your clients should sign up for the auto bill to their credit card thereby racking up frequent flyer miles or rebates. Write down all of their credit card information including the card verification number on the back. You might want to write this down on something other than the estimate form.

Since your teams will be trained to leave a note on the kitchen counter, ask the customer to leave the check there if that is the option they prefer.

## Operations

Your objective is to staff and maintain regular cleaning/homemaking crews in your area. Your team leader will be your Schedule Manager and you will pay them more. You can do this by-the-hour and reimburse for gas mileage, or pay a percentage of the job or jobs (22-

23%) and supply the vehicle. Piece rate is the best way to go. (See chapter __ on piece rate)

Your supervisor would be responsible for driving, collecting checks, leaving invoices and leaving client notes. They are also responsible for turning in odometer readings for the day (if you pay by the mile), times in and out of the houses, noting who did wet and dry chores in each home and finally, making sure the team's kit and equipment is stocked.

Your Associate or Homemakers (HA) assist the supervisor but is also a cleaner.

When starting your cleaning program you will probably need only one cleaner. He/she should be able to clean two homes a day. Tell clients how busy you are and schedule according. For example your cleaner will have a 10:00am to 1:00p clean. The next clean will be from 2:00p to 5:00p.

Ten consistent cleans a week is excellent to begin. By doing so you will be able to monitor how the cleaner does and call clients to receive feedback.

When you reach ten consistent cleans, it will be time to hire a supervisor who will also be a cleaner.

I think a good short-term goal would be to clean 25 clients per week with a longer vision of 50 clients per week.

## Responsibility of Supervisors

Hiring and firing

Training cleaners

Inspect homes

Maintain cleaning supplies

All scheduling

Have all work books in order and complete


## What to look for in a Supervisor

How do they present themselves?

Are they neatly dressed?

Do they take control when doing a clean?

Do they work independently?

They may not be your best cleaner, but are always willing to do whatever is asked

DON'T HIRE THE BEAUTIFUL PEOPLE (meaning they don't use elbow grease and aren't willing to get their hands dirty they won't be cleaners)

## What's a Work Book?

A plastic three hole folder

On the outside of the folder you need the (Your Company Name) name and your cleaner's name.

MSD sheets on all the basic cleaning chemicals you carry in your cleaning kit.

Company insurance paper and bonded information

Weekly calendar

Work Order sheets with information for the clean

MapQuest for new clients

Several blank work order papers in case you're out on the road and have an unexpected clean

A credit card bill authorization paper, if client would like to charge to credit card

¼ pad to write a personal note to the client.

Several pens

Maintenance of the Work Book is the Supervisor's responsibility.

## Office Books

There will be several books that you need to maintain in your office:

Current Customer book- Your Current Customer book includes your permanent cleaning instructions. It should also include your copy of the estimate sheet and rotational chore sheet.

Estimates done, but "did not close" book- Your estimates done but "did not close" book should include your copy of the estimate sheet/rotational chore sheet/driving instructions.

Former Customers book- Move current customers out of the current customer book into this book when they do a p.c. (permanent cancel). You will get call backs to re-start the service.

MSD Master Log book- Your MSD Master Log book should contain MSD sheets for every cleaning product you go out in the field with. You need to have and maintain this by law. If you have a client that wants us to use one of their cleaning items, we need to look the item over and contact the manufacturer for an MSD sheet. They are required by law to send us out that information.

## Other Considerations

Courtesy Calls - Place Courtesy Calls the day before the cleaning to your clients. It's a great customer service tool and it will cut down on your temporary cancellation rate. You can also do this to confirm your appointments for an estimate. The farther out you set the appointment the greater chance there is on them canceling. Nothing worse to be ringing a doorbell no one will ever answer while you could be doing another revenue producing activity.

**Storage Area** - Have an area to stash workbooks, vacuums and cleaning kits and set up your chemical dispensers. You will need to locate your chemical dispenser near a source of water, if you do not have access to water use the 2-1/2 gallon containers along with their pump. In this storage area you will need a first aid chart, first aid kit, and your MSDS chemical notebook to meet OSHA requirements.

**Vacuum Waiver**

Have your client sign a vacuum waiver that we are not responsible if it breaks nor are we responsible for changing water/bags or filters. (Chapter 10 Forms.)

**Supplies**

Always be shopping around for supplies to see who has the best price.

Your cleaning supplies should total no more are than two percent of your gross sales.

I have used Ecolab Products in the past. I recommend that if you do not have Ecolab in your area that you contact a local cleaning chemical supply company and price their products.

Ecolab products are used by most major hotel chains and cleaning services. Ecolab will supply you with the cleaning products as well as spray bottles, nozzles and labels. Products will be delivered to your home office. You will need to set up a rack near water for the concentrated products.

I would recommend your Ecolab starter kit should consist of:

Oasis Pro 16 Orange Force multi-surface (cleaner and de-greaser in one)

Oasis Pro 41 Glass Cleaner (Very strong)

14 Antibacterial All-Purpose Cleaner (works great in kitchens)

ECOLAB sells other products you may want to consider including "green" products. Make sure the products you select are cost effective.

For Eco friendly items we suggest: 20 Mule Team Borax, Bon Ami, Vinegar, and Baking Soda.

On all cleaning products, spray and let stand for a couple of minutes (5). Let the cleaner work for you.

When ordering from Ecolab products make sure they send you the stickers related to the chemicals you will be using. The stickers have to be placed on every spray bottle. They will also send you the MSDS papers.

Do not use paper towels to clean! Use cloth diapers. You can purchase cloth diapers by ordering directly from a vendor or at a local diaper delivery service. You may be able to negotiate a lower price on seconds; diapers that can no longer be used because of wear and tear, but still work great as cleaning rags. These are usually available in

February.

Don't throw away your shredded and beat up towels. You will need 6-8 of these for oven cleaning. They will be ready to throw out by the time you're through cleaning the oven.

## General Products

The following items should also be purchased for your cleaning starter kit:

- Bucket
- Scrubbies (found at a janitorial supply. Get the white and cut them into thirds)
- Roll of waste basket liners
- Broom and dust pan
- Extender duster (found at Wal-Mart)
- Latex gloves
- Cloth Towels
- A standard size scrub brush, It looks like a toothbrush size scrub brush
- Spray bottles (the longest lasting ones are found at a janitorial supply)
- Large size plastic cup (used to wash down shower walls)

Other items that you may need to stock include: Oven Cleaning (Easy Off), hard water removal (pink power found in janitorial supply) and a pumice stone for cleaning hard water from the toilet bowls. Make sure to get an MSD sheet on each one. Release these items as needed. Review use with your team. Have these items turned back in at the end of the day.

The Eco Labs All Purpose Cleaner is very effective in the kitchen.

If you allow vinegar to stand on the glass for a few minutes it will take off the hard water stains. It is also good for cleaning hardwood floors. We suggest that the cleaner asks the home owner if they have special products she could use for cleaning their hardwood floors.

If the senior wants their furniture waxed they have their own wax they prefer.

When mopping floors we usually do them on our hands and knees. If the floors are tile we use the all purpose cleaner diluted with hot water and our broom to scrub the floors. Then with the towels we rinse and dry.

Your white scrubbies can be washed and are great for the kitchen and bathrooms. They are not abrasive so they won't scratch stainless steel sink or a glass top stove.  You can buy these at any janitorial supply place. We general cut these into thirds. About every two weeks they will need to be replaced.

Never mix chemicals-you can create "knock out" fumes if mixing ammonia base chemicals with other chemicals.


Bring dirty cleaning rags back into the office so the supervisor can clean them. That way we have quality control. Usually we place our dirty rags in a trash liner bag.

Your cleaning supply total should be no more than 2% of gross sales.
Your cleaning equipment total should be around 3.5% of gross sales.

## Equipment/Supplies

## Vacuum Cleaner

You need to start with one vacuum. It is suggested that you use the
home owners vacuum so you won't contaminate or bring any unwanted
germs into their home. When evaluating a vacuum cleaner purchase
think in terms of never taking it to a vacuum repair shop and on
minimizing ongoing costs. The most cost effective vacuum is the
commercial grade Santaire upright. They do not have bags and all parts
are replaceable.

## Cleaning Tips

Always start furthest from your exist point.

When cleaning a bathroom with carpets place an old towel on the floor
to protect the carpet and if you don't have a large towel place your
hucks on the floor.

If two cleaners are working together, they should discuss what each
other will clean before entering the home. I recommend that one works
on the top floor while the other works the other level.

Cleaners should not climb ladders. Let the client know it's against OSHA.

If you are cleaning specialty items ask the client if they have special cleaning products for these items.

I like using brooms for scrubbing tile or vinyl floors then wipe dry

Floor boards should always be dusted

Clients always check corners so make sure they're clean

## Field Estimating Kit Materials

Presentation Book

1- Green 3-ring binder with inside pockets.  3-hole punched plastic sheets, piece of 8 ½ x 11, 3-hole punched chipboard inserts.

Estimating Book

1- Green 3-ring binder with inside pockets.  3-hole punched plastic sheets, piece of 8 ½ x 11, 3-hole punched chipboard inserts.

## Employees

Employees will be you biggest challenge in any service-based businesses.  Don't let it stop you.  Your future employee is out there now either not working or working.  For those working many are involved with retail or fast food places that are open nights and weekends.

Our position is a blue-collar job with white-collar hours.  Many of these people can make as much, if not more, working for you, than where they are at now.  They can have dinner with their family every night and do things with them on the weekend.  You get to these folks through the classified ads.  Figure out which of the free publications you can get some results from in your local market.

Reach out to your Hispanic community.  Find out where they go to church or where they go shopping.  Don't give up if you don't have instant success.  If you can become a preferable employer in your area, you should get plenty of referrals from your existing employees.  In the Hispanic community, they have large extended families and it is important that mom is home at night.

**Initial Training**

Have a formalized training session you are putting your new employees through.  Have them fill out ALL of the appropriate paperwork and set up an employee file.

Application, Federal and state withholding

I-9

Acknowledgement of Employee Handbook

Non-Compete agreement

Authorization for a Background check

Uniform Receipt

Have your team clean your house under your supervision.

Go through the cleaning chemicals, equipment, workbook, and your office protocol.

Once you are up and going, identify a supervisor and send your new employees out to be trained by them. They will let you know if you have the "right" employee.

**Employee Tips**

I highly recommend setting up a continental breakfast for your employees, if this is feasible. Just some simple things like coffee, bagels, margarine, jelly and peanut butter. It also goes a long way when the boss passes out paychecks on Friday mornings. It is also a good day to have a short staff meeting.

**Other tips:**

Always recognize birthdays and service anniversaries!!!! A certificate on the wall, a birthday card and cake go a long way!

Always ask for input from your field staff and reward and recognize implemented ideas.

Take away any us vs. them mentality that sometimes exists in this industry.

# Yard Care

Lawn mowing and yard care can be a valuable add-on service for your business and senior care clients that wish to stay in their home.

**Lawn Mowing**

Lawn Care is the general cutting, trimming and maintenance of a lawn or property and whatever else that lies on the lawn and its surroundings.

## How Much to Charge for Lawn Mowing

First off, set a lawn mowing "drop gate" fee which should be $25 - $30.00. Do not make exceptions. This is the fee for showing up to the customers' house, and "dropping" the gate. It is a minimum service charge.

Most of your small residential accounts fall in the range of $30-$40. When determining the bid you have to take into account multiple aspects before giving them the quote. Depending on the location, how many other clients you have in the area, the house, the personality of the client, the amount of quality you think the customer will expect, etc, then you can give them the quote. Also take into account the size of the lawn, obstacles (I.E toys, trees, rocks, hills) and areas that may take more time. (I.E areas you can't fit a big mower in and have to push mow) As a rough guide, a $30 lawn should take your crew approximately 10-15 minutes, a $40 lawn 15-25 minutes, and a $50 lawn 25- 40 minutes. From there, the price goes up. If a customer requests a bi-weekly mow, and it is a reasonable request (on a slow growing lawn) then allow it, but usually charge a bit extra.

Finally, shoot high on the price. Giving a higher price allows room for bargaining on the customers end.  People tend to negotiate if you give your bottom line price first you have no room to bargain with the client. Also, if you give the high price first and they don't negotiate, you get more for the property, so it's a win-win situation.

## How Much Money can you make?

Lawn care and landscape maintenance can be very profitable. The key to your profitability is as follows:

Pay your employees on a piece rate system not to exceed 30% of the total amount of the invoiced job.  Example, you bill a job for $75 and it takes one full hour for the job to be completed by two employees.  The total amount of available dollars to be paid to the employees for that job is $18.75 at 25% of the total invoiced amount.  The employees will be paid $9.37 each for the lawn.  It is important to remember that lawn employees are use to being paid minimum wage or by piece rate.  Piece rate encourages the employees to cut more lawns per hour, per day because it financially rewards them for production.  On the contrary, paying the employee hourly rewards them for doing as little as possible in an eight hour day.  An average team of two employees on piece rate should be able to cut approximately 20-25 houses a day. Of course, this depends on the size of the lawn and the traveling distance between lawn cuts.  Please see Chapter 7 for more information on Piece Rate.

Schedule properties to be cut as close together on the same day as possible.  This will increase your efficiency and cut down on lost travel time.

Make sure you bid properly.

You need to establish a minimum amount for showing up to cut a lawn. Some lawns will only take 10-15 minutes to cut but it is not profitable to show up to a lawn and cut it for $18.75.  We recommend that you have a minimum of a 30 minute charge of $35 -$37.50

## Senior Clients

### Getting to know the Clients needs

It is very important that before you begin mowing for the season your staff is aware of how each client likes their lawn mowed.  Many professional mowing companies make the mistake of mowing their client's lawns the way they think it should be mowed instead of how the client wants it mowed.

If you choose to provide lawn services you will be dealing with many senior citizen clients.  Seniors tend to be more particular about how their yard is maintained and how their lawn is mowed.  It is important to remember that they have been maintaining their yard in a certain way for many years.  Also, they may have a certain routine, for example, they may edge the lawn before they mow or they mow their lawn every

Thursday morning at 10:00 a.m. It is important that every consideration is made to accommodate these routines when setting up schedules and yard care plans.

**Performing the service**

Upon arriving at the clients home the lead member of the crew must knock on the client's door and let the client know that they are going to perform the service. (This step can be omitted if the home is vacant; no senior is present or the client requests.) The lead member **must ask at this time** if there is anything special the client wants done with regards to the lawn or yard.

Most often the client will just acknowledge that you are there and let you begin mowing. However, sometimes they may ask for some additional items to be addressed. This could range from simple items like blowing dust and grass off of their outdoor furniture to more time intensive requests like weeding flower beds. It is important that your lawn crew accommodate the simple requests as long as it does not interfere with their schedule. More time intensive requests should immediately be called into the office so that you can schedule a yard cleanup crew to handle the request.

After visiting briefly with the client, the lawn crew should immediately begin to mow and edge the lawn. The lawn should be mowed to the specifications set out in the yard care plan. After mowing, the crew member responsible for mowing the lawn needs to give the lawn a once over to make sure no blades of grass were missed and that all wheel lines are straight. Any imperfections must be rectified before leaving.

Edging and trimming is the frame that makes the picture. A perfectly mowed lawn will never look good if the edges are left shaggy. In your lawn care manual you should require that all perimeters of the lawn be edged. Edging and trimming should take place around all trees, decorative curbing, play equipment, statues, etc. Cracks in the driveway, along walkways and sidewalks should also be trimmed with the power trimmer.

After the lawn has been mowed, edged and trimmed it is important that all areas be blown free of grass clippings. As part of the service it is necessary that the crew blow off all sidewalks, driveways, patios and porches before leaving. All grass clippings should be blown into a pile and removed from the property. **Under no circumstances should clippings be blown into the street.**

Finally, before leaving, **the lead crew member** should check to make sure all service items have been performed properly and that all equipment is placed safely back on the trailer or truck. The lead crew member must then knock on the client's door and make sure the client is satisfied with the service.

## Yard Maintenance

Yard care maintenance will also be a popular service for seniors and it can be a very lucrative part of your business. This is an area that most seniors have a difficult time with. It also presents a serious risk of fall or injury to seniors.

The following is a synopsis of yard maintenance services and how to perform them.

### Spring clean-ups

Spring clean-ups include leaf removal, bed preparation, trash or debris removal, bush and small tree trimming, plant flowers (provided by client), weeding and placement of outdoor furniture, etc. These clean-ups should be scheduled as soon as the majority of snow has melted. In climates where no snow is present or there is year round yard services these clean-ups can be performed monthly, quarterly, semi-annually or yearly depending on the clients wishes.

### Fall Clean-ups

Fall clean-ups include leaf, trash and debris removal, clean out beds, trim bushes and small trees, cover or store outdoor furniture, etc. Fall clean-ups are utilized in areas with distinct seasons. This service should be scheduled during the months of September, October and November.

### Monthly/Bi-weekly yard maintenance

Scheduled yard maintenance throughout the season is an excellent way to keep your crews busy and increase your bottom line. Many seniors are use to having their yards kept in tip top shape. This type of service usually includes weeding, trimming of bushes, planting of flowers, edging, debris removal and some limited fertilization.

### How to bid yard maintenance and clean-up services

It is very important to bid yard maintenance services appropriately. These services can be very profitable if bid properly or they can be financially taxing if they are bid wrong. Unfortunately, since there are so many variables when bidding a yard clean-up service, such as the depth and dampness of leaves, height and thickness of weeds, size and quantity of fallen branches, number of beds to be weeded or planted, contour of yard, obstacles, etc, that there is no way to develop a standard pricing matrix for determining price. It is important to know how quickly your crews can perform these services and then bid these jobs by the hour.

I recommend that you charge between $25 and $30 an hour for yard maintenance services per employee. An average clean-up for a .24 acre lot with home on it should take 3-4 hours for two guys. (Example, 4 hours x 2 employees = 8 hours. 8 x $30 = $240). **IMPORTANT do not forget the dump fees!** Make sure that you add the dump fees and the hours to drive to the dump and empty your load to the final bill. If you can do several jobs before you have to go to the dump, factor that in and divide up the cost of the dump fee amongst all the clients that day. I recommend that you contact your local dump to determine pricing for your area to insure accuracy when pricing. For example:

**$240 service cost**

**$55 dump fee ($25 for the dump and $30 for an hour of labor.**

**Total = $295**

Leaf clean up on the ground can be accomplished by either using your blowers or by using rakes. Blowers can be used effectively by blowing all of the leaves up into a pile and then place them into large garbage bags or tarps. Tarps are recommended to help cut down on the cost of purchasing bags. Many clients may have a compost pile and they may request you place the leaves and grass clippings into their compost. It is important to ask before commencing with the job. Placement in compost piles will also reduce your need to go to the dump and will save space in your garbage dumpster.

The time it takes to clean up leaves can vary due to rain, tall grass, leaves from neighbor's yards, etc. Because of these issues it is recommend that these jobs be charged by the hour.

# CHAPTER 7

# Control Your Labor-Control Your Life

## Controlling Labor Production Pay/Piece Rate

### Controlling Labor Production Pay/Piece Rate

Let me tell you an all too common story. The early 2000's were a dream come true for home owners, business owners, business executives as it seemed like anything we produced, it sold. Any business that was going well prior to 2000, improved by leaps and bounds. Credit was easy to establish. Buy now, pay later! Purchase a second, third home with equity from another home. Consumers were excited to spend. Investors were coming out of the woods and everything was working so well. It just felt the sky was the limit.

My business coach told me a story that has stuck with me all these years. The business coach was introduced to an owner of a large HVAC company. This particular company sold air condition and heating units to residential homes. They also maintained the units. The owner let him know that they were installing an average of 45 units per week for over 10 years in a row. In two particular years, the company averaged over 60 units per week. The company invested heavily in equipment, training and tools to manage this company. The company owned 17 vans for installation and repair. The teams were working 40-50 hours per week and the company was making a lot of revenue and the profits were good enough to put away $50-60,000 per month in the business operations fund. The crews were like family to this owner and he simply didn't mind paying overtime because the profits were good. The owner felt as if he had achieved his dreams and couldn't imagine the business doing anything but well.

The business started to change back in 2008 when the economy started to change. This business owner felt as if he could probably withstand a slight drop in the economy as he had a large operations fund ($1.2 million) and didn't imagine this dip in business to last more than a season or two. He felt that he had such a great team and together they would all pull through this downturn.

It's now 2012 and the business is currently in bankruptcy and his largest creditor is selling off vehicles, equipment and the inventory. Gone is the $1.2 million in operations capital, the large line of credit and the owner is back in a van repairing equipment. The owner did not go out of business but he did step back 20 years and has very little to show for it. He is currently 57 years of age. He doesn't anticipate being able to retire for another 20 years.

The following information will help you and your business avoid the same type of tragedy. Hopefully you will be inspired and see the warning signs.

## Why Did You Go Into Business?

One of the first questions a business owner should ask themselves is why they chose their profession and what is their expectation? Many people are not meant to be business owners and many are not called to be employees. How did we get here? Now that you are here, what is your expectation and do you have a strong enough "why" to get you to get off your duff? Did you go in business to pay others or did you go into business for yourself?

## Buying Your Clients

Too many business owners don't understand the cost of going into business. I would rather buy an existing business and make it better instead of buying a new business.

The biggest reason why so many businesses fail is they don't understand acquisition costs of new clients. Acquisition cost is what it cost you to get a new client. **Example:** If you spent $2,000 on a marketing piece and you received 20 new clients out of this piece, your acquisition cost is now $100 per customer. That is wonderful if your service or product is a high ticket item or your product/service is something that is ongoing. It is not so good for the owner if your product/service is a one-time purchase and the purchase was less than the acquisition cost.

I mentioned that that the biggest reason why so many businesses fail is they don't understand acquisition costs. If you do the math and your acquisition cost is $25 per client and your business needs 1,000 clients to hit your break even mark, your marketing costs will need to exceed $25,000. When most small businesses start up, they normally don't budget $25,000 for marketing and then they wonder why they fail.

One of the key elements of creating a great business is figuring out how to lower your acquisition cost and increase the lifetime value of your clients. The only way you can lower your acquisition cost is by measuring everything and getting better. Try out new marketing pieces and measures which ones give the most bang for your buck.

## Save Your Business

The information so far has been simply to set the tone:

- Nobody cares about your business as much as you.
- Employees waste 30% of your time and money doing unproductive items.
- When your business has a downturn, you'll find that your staff simply wants to be paid and doesn't care if you are paid.
- You went into business for yourself, not everyone else.
- You must understand what a customer is worth to your business.
- Labor is your number one cost.

Saving your business comes down to two items: 1. Continuous marketing 2. Controlling all of your costs. Being that labor is your number one cost, the rest of this information booklet has to do with the nuts and bolts of where you can control labor and how to do it.

# CHAPTER 8

# PIECE RATE

This chapter will explain piece rate. As I stated in previous chapters, it is not suggested that you use piece rate to pay your senior care employees. However, if you are going to have value added services with employees performing the work then piece rate is the only way to go.

**Introduction to Piece Rate**

What's the incentive for your staff on hourly rate? None! Individual incentive plans offer the clearest link between a worker's effort and the reward. Probably the best known individual or small group incentive pay plan is *piece rate*. Piece rate had been more suited to repetitive crew work (e.g., housekeeping, lawn cuts, etc) than to office work. As the tie between individual work and results is diminished, so is the motivating effect of the incentive on the individual.

My background is growing business, controlling costs and helping individuals across the country realize the dream of owning a business. Most of my education comes from my college background and years of testing and measuring. I have built businesses and have used these techniques to become more profitable. According to Randall Bartlett at Smith College, there are six principles of human behavior accepted by economists for making decisions:

1. People Respond to Incentives
2. No Free Lunch Due to Scarcity
3. Must Know the Opportunity Cost of Any Decision
4. All Actions Have Unintended Consequences
5. One Never Can do Just One Thing
6. Nobody Is Truly in Control

The objective of this introduction is to summarize much of this work, and give clear and precise suggestions for the effective design of piece rate pay and controlling your labor costs. A number of serious challenges that threaten the effectiveness of this pay method are also included. While my work has been primarily in cleaning and handyman, the principles can be easily adapted to other types of work.

Gregorio Billikoff wrote on his thesis; I was taken aback by the assertion of a colleague at the University of California, Davis, "Civilized nations," he argued, "have moved away from paying by the piece." Certainly, there are articles and papers on the death of piece rate. While piece rate is still utilized widely, it often fails to motivate employees as much as it could. Greed—on both sides—often gets in the way. Traditionally both the employer and worker have come to believe that the other is out to cheat him. Piece rate, rightfully so, is often associated with a game played between the two.

Employers can build piece rate systems that prevent workers from earning higher wages at the expense of the enterprise. But just as important, employers can (and should) design piece rate approaches that help build worker motivation and trust. What is at stake is a sustainable pay system with the potential to greatly benefit both employer and employee in the long run. Owners can reduce costs while increasing productivity. Workers can earn substantially greater amounts. Such enterprises are likely to have a waiting list of excellent people who wish to work for them and have little to worry when talk of labor shortages are raised.

When we're dealing with employees, framing and reframing are important aspects of negotiation—of viewing issues from a particular perspective. I always ask my employees, "How would you feel if some of your crew workers made twice the minimum wage and you still made money? Without fail the answer is that this would be great. "How about three times the minimum wage?" I inquired next. "Would that make you nervous?"

The fact of the matter is that your staff can and will make a lot more if and when Piece Rate is implemented properly. Certainly, the very thought of your staff earning three or more times the minimum wage would send some business owners straight to the trauma center. The owners are likely to feel that they made a mistake when they set up their piece rate. One need to reframe, then, has to do with the bottom line. Instead of panicking at the hourly equivalent that a piece-rate paid worker is earning, look at the bottom line such as cost per lawn, cost per house cleaned, cost per loaf, cost per square ft., etc.

Put another way, in the form of a question: "Does your company make more money as your staff makes more money?" If the answer is a 'maybe' or a 'no,' your pay for performance design is faulty. If the answer is a 'yes,' why worry because some of your staff is going home with their pockets full of money?

I spoke earlier about framing and reframing are aspects of negotiation. They are also aspects of trust. Once your staff starts making a good living, some of your staff will be nervous that you will cut their piece-rate pay—either now or next year—if they perform at their full potential. Some owners who have understood and overcome this trust issue have had employees make three times the minimum wage and more.

As the business owners must:

1. Find the right piece rate percentage.
2. Communicate it to the staff.
3. Find the staff enough work to make a decent living.
4. Bid properly.
5. Don't change the percentage. Also, don't start the piece rate too high. Once you start it too high, you can't go back easily. Without a doubt, nothing can kill worker motivation faster than having the piece rate lowered—or the fear of the same.

Starting the process of piece rate requires a degree of boldness especially for those that were paid hourly wages from the commencement of your business. Be prepared to lose staff because it will happen. Everyone "knows" someone that was on piece rate of production pay that was "cheated" out of pay. Some simply won't give it a chance and will leave immediately. Some will start the process and won't see the vision of the earning potential or don't understand the value of additional time and will leave. For those that stick it out, confidence and trust will build over time for both sides.

Once you make the commitment, stay with it! The price for being consistent will pay off for your staff and your business!

## Where Can I Control My Labor?

The simple answer to that question is everywhere. The fact of the matter is that all jobs including office staff can be controlled:

- Housekeeping – Percentage of the job
- Handyman – Percentage of the job
- Yard Care – Percentage of the job
- Supervisor/Manager for any department. Small salary plus incentives to grow their departments.
- Subcontractors – Percentage of the job.
- Office Staff – Set the hours.
- Elder Care – Elder Care is normally paid by the hour so you simply pay your staff by the same amount of hours that you bill. The job starts and ends on the site of the patient.
- Medical Care – Paid by the patient
- Sales – Small salary plus commission for short period of time until small salary is taken away.

## How Do I Control My Labor?

Controlling labor is quite simple but we as business owners like to make it too difficult. There is always a reason, "why it won't work." The fact of the matter is that it does work in 95% of all situations. The only time it doesn't work at is when all of your work orders are spread hours apart. In that case, the business owner must bid for the travel time or find part time workers/contractors to do each job individually in the different areas and paid a percentage of the job.

Piece rate stems from the premises that your workers are only guaranteed minimum wage for their time. Let me repeat that part. All employees are minimum wage employees and must sign a document stating such. All employees must keep track of their time. Dollars earned at the end of the week must be divided into the hours worked. If your staff does not earn enough in the week to be paid minimum wage, you must pay them the difference. Piece rate is also a great filter. If your staff only earns minimum wage, you don't want them but they usually quit first after they get their first check.

As the business owner, your main responsibility is to find work and to train. Be sure to adequately train your employees using your own manuals and be sure to have contracts and agreements in place.

**Percentages:** Remember that your staff and your business are only as good as your bid. You want to pay your staff a great wage. If you are the lowest guy in town, you won't be able to pay a good wage and your staff will leave you. Educate your customer and give them value. You absolutely cannot be the lowest bidder in town. If you live by price, you will die by price! Stay away from price strategies and concentrate on education and value added services.

The following is a list of labor percentages for cleaning jobs:

|  | **Excellent** | **Marginal** | **Poor** |
| --- | --- | --- | --- |
| Cleaning | Less than 26% | 27-35% | Over 35% |

**Administrative:**

Many times administrative costs can go through the roof. Many companies bring someone on from the inception of the business. If this is the case for your company, make sure that the administrative person allows you to Market and Train your staff. If you find that you are spending too much time doing administrative items, you have the wrong person. You want to get to a place where your administrative labor is 6% or less of your total revenue. Your administrative person needs to know that they will be required to do everything in the office from answering telephones, ordering supplies, cleaning, assigning work orders, taking payment, finances, motivating, marketing, following up, etc. If you hire an administrative person from the inception, they must be thought of as an investment so that you can get out to market and train. Your 6% ratio needs to come into line within 6 months or you should cut the hours.

Another way to control your administrative person is simply allow that person to work based on revenue. **Example:** If you have scheduled $5,000 in business that week, divide the $5,000 by 6% = $300. If you pay your administrative person $11 per hour, he/she will have 27 1/4 hours

($11 x 27.25 hrs. = $299.75) of available time to work that week. The right person will be motivated to help find more work and motivate the owners to get out there so that you can increase the admin hours. Many companies will use the same guide but pay the hours the following week as many times it is difficult to determine how much revenue is scheduled before the week starts.

Your administrative people are there to make things run better and for you to look better. If your administrative persons don't make you a better owner and your staff better, you have the wrong person.

**Supervisors** are similar to administrative people. Supervisors are not "divas" or "bosses" in the sense that when you start a business, they must be working supervisors. Supervisors should not be retained until the owner is in a place where bidding and working interfere with each other. Hire a Supervisor after the bidding ration takes up half their work time per week. The reason is because that is the point where the owner is earning enough that it doesn't make sense for the owner to be actually working on the job because his/her hourly rate is to a point that bidding brings in 4 to 5 times more in revenue than one would be paid to do the work. If an owner is bringing in more than $55 an hour for finding work, why would the owner ever do work that he/she could pay someone $10-15 an hour to perform?

Supervisors are under the same scrutiny as normal staff. They are still paid piece rate for the jobs they are doing and should not be made Supervisors until there is more than 40 hours a week of work.

While the business is still in its infancy, the owners may be required to have staff doing some of the bidding. The problem that could occur is that under the "piece rate" system, your staff does not get paid to do bids because bidding is not a paid job. For this reason, it sometimes becomes necessary to give an allowable payment to your Supervisors so that they can find work.

**Example:** While growing any department, it would make sense to pay a weekly "salary" of $320. This will guarantee a full time Supervisor earns a minimum of $8 an hour for a 40 hour work week. If the Supervisor earns more than $320 from piece rate while working, we pay the Supervisor the greater amount. (Set $320 or money earned from working)  During the Supervisor's slow time each day, they may be doing bids, passing out flyers, marketing, following up on leads, etc. You must have set expectations as well. When passing out flyers, it is expected that they track where they deliver and hand out a minimum of 85 flyers per hour.  There becomes a point with the Supervisor that you they will be doing more administrative, training, following up on leads, hiring, discipline and bidding that pull the Supervisors away from doing actual work. In those cases, it is best to set up fees for each of their activities.

The Supervisor should always receive the greater amount from the work or salary but would be incentivized to do the other aspects of their job. The above-mentioned are simply recommendations. Your Supervisors are working Supervisors and are not to be in the office for very much time. The only reasons for your Supervisors to be in the office more than a half hour per day is because you are training them, they are training a staff member or they are creating a bid or marketing piece.

Keep track of your Supervisor's time and do not allow them to get comfortable for any reason. It's ok if your Supervisor earns over $50k annually. That means they helped bring in four to five times more in their department.

**Paying Mileage:**

As a rule of thumb, do not pay mileage. On occasion, staff members use their own vehicles. It is not recommended because they might not have the proper insurance and if they wreck into another car or do personal damage, your insurance many not cover them and you may be headed into a lawsuit. If someone used their vehicle for work, it is better to pay them a gas stipend rather than mileage. **Example:** pay someone $50 per week if they use their equipment as an employee. Don't pay contractors any sort of mileage. I saw one business owner pay .40 cents per mile. The employee drove nearly 200 miles per day and the employer ended up paying hundreds of dollars per week. In one case, the owner was paying out nearly $1,000 per week. It would have been less expensive to buy three new vehicles and pay for all fill ups, repairs and oil changes. Don't get caught in this trap because your profit will go straight down the drain.

**Payroll**:

One of the questions that arise is: How do I keep the labor board out of my office? That is a great question and will come up from your staff without fail. Most of your staff has not worked under piece rate and may feel that we are "ripping them off". It is an easy fix.

All staff members **MUST** track their hours. We don't pay overtime. Everyone is hired as a minimum wage employee. Rather than pay overtime, hire an additional staff member that starts early in the afternoon.

Overtime will kill your margins. Everyone tracks their labor. At the end of each week, you simply divide all "piece rate" dollars earned by their amount of hours worked. **Example:** Your handyman earns $600 and works 30 hours during that week. The time includes their travel time. This means your handyman earned $20 per hour. ($600 divided by 30 hours = $20 per hour)  As the employer, you must 1) track dollars earned an average hourly rate for the week and 2) a running total for the year.  If the labor board shows up, you simply showed them that they earned more than minimum wage. In most every single case, your staff will be earning more than the local average hourly rate. As you learn to bid, your staff will earn more than the average hourly rate.

# CHAPTER 9

# HIPPA OVERVIEW

## HIPPA WORKBOOK

## Introduction

HIPPA stands for the Health Insurance Portability & Accountability Act of 1996. The HIPPA rule has several parts. This workbook will cover the part that protects the privacy of medical records and information of our clients.

It limits the use and sharing of health information. It gives patients several rights related to their information. It requires we limit what is released to the least amount needed. Abuse of information is subject to criminal and civil penalties.

This affects all of our clients no matter who is paying the bill.

I will go over how the company will handle the rule and steps you will need to take to comply.

## Protected Information

The rule protects information related to a client's health. This includes:

- Patient name and geographic subdivision
- Birth Date
- Telephone and Fax number

- E-mail address and URL addresses
- Social Security number
- Medical record number
- Insurance number and Account numbers
- License or certificate number
- License plate number and Vehicle identification number (VIN)
- Equipment and device identifier and serial number
- Photograph, voice or finger prints
- Diagnosis, condition and treatment
- Any other number that could be used to identify information

Think of health information as your credit card. Most people see their credit card information as private and take steps to protect it. You would not put your credit card on a bulletin board or leave the card on your desk while you are out to lunch. You wouldn't leave your credit card on the front seat of your car or on your kitchen table when you have company. Client information is the same. You must protect your client's information so that someone else does not accidentally see or hear the information.

You would provide this information to certain people who need the information. For example, if you lost your card, you would share the card number, your social security number, and any other necessary information with your credit card company so that they could send you a replacement. The following pages will explain when you can and cannot share your client's personal information.

# How Client Information Can and Cannot Be Used

As a home care company, you use protected client information daily. It is important to know how you can and cannot use your client's information.

Using protected patient information is a part of what you do. As a care provider you will use protected client information in the following ways.

## Treatment

You can use or share information in order to provide care to your client. This includes talking to doctors or other people providing care to the client. You can also share information when arranging for others to care for the client. For example, you can share information necessary to order Meals on Wheels for your client. Sometimes you also need to talk with other company employees. If this is about the care of your client, it is OK.

### Payment

You can use information so that you get paid for the services you provide.

### Care Operations

You can use information in activities as a business

Clinical record reviews

Care plan development, managing cases and coordinating **Care**

Looking at caregiver's notes as part of yearly review

Training programs

Sharing client information during a survey

Reviews and audits, including compliance reviews and **Medical reviews**

Planning and developing business

Patient satisfaction surveys

Emergency and disaster planning and implementation

Performing general office functions

When legal services are needed you can share information regarding the issue

How you use client information depends on your job. A caregiver will not use it in the same way as a billing office manager. For example a caregiver will use the information to prepare meals while the billing office will use the information for reimbursement.

## Guidelines for Use

- Inform clients – before you can use any protected patient information, you must let the client know how you are using it. To do this, you must give each client a Notice of Information and Privacy Practices. This form must be given to all clients when you are responsible for overseeing their care. This is determined if you have them sign a service agreement. You will give them the form when you start their care. It tells the client how you will use and share their protected information.

- Use companies that agree to follow the rules – Sometimes you will use people not employed by the company to do things for you. They are called Business Associates. You must have an agreement with them stating that they will follow the rules. If you have this agreement, you can share information with them when providing care for your clients.

- Limit information – whenever you use information or give information to others you have to be careful. Be sure to limit the amount of information to the least amount possible. This is true for every situation, including those in which it is OK for you to use information. Remember the credit care example? You shared the card number with the credit card company because it was needed to replace your card. However, if you were telling a friend that you lost the card, there is no reason to share the card number with your friend because your friend does not need this information.

- Remove specific information – if you take away all the pieces of information that would tell you who the client is, you can use the information for any purpose. These elements were outlined in the protected information section you read earlier in this workbook. For example, if you wanted to write a report on clients with diabetes, remove the protected information. Then you could share the report with anyone as it tells you information about clients, in general, who have diabetes.

- Electronic communication – electronic communication must also be protected. Client information cannot be listed in any e-mail that is sent via the internet. If the e-mail is sent within the company's network (intranet) limit client information and do not include the client's name in the subject line. If you need to send a file with client information via the internet, the file must be password protected.

- Verbal communication – additionally, verbal communication must be protected. This does not mean everyone must have a private office to discuss client information; it means lower the volume of your voice when discussing client information.

Client information cannot be used for anything other than what was just discussed.

## Authorization to Release Information

If you want to use protected information for something else, you must get the client's written authorization. For example, if you wanted to present information about a specific client's case at a national clinical conference, you would need authorization to share the client's name and other protected information. The authorization must include the reason for the release. It must tell you who will receive the information and if you were paid to share it.

An authorization is also required in order to use or share information for the purpose of sales and marketing. Protected information should not be shared with sales representatives for the sole purpose of increasing referrals.

The client can refuse to let you share their information. Refusing to share information cannot affect their care. After a client gives their authorization, they can take it back at any time.

We have to give the client a copy of the authorization. The location must keep the authorization in the client's clinical record. It should never be moved to a thinned chart.

**Psychiatric Notes**

Information created by a mental health professional must be handled differently. This includes information that evaluates discussions during a counseling session. You must obtain special permission to use their information, even for ways that are okay for others. This does not include when you are monitoring medications or their effectiveness at controlling a behavior. It also does not include the client's progress or summary of symptoms. The care your home care providers are providing does not need to be treated separately.

## How to Prevent Releasing Information by Mistake

Sometimes, the sharing of protected client information is not on purpose. Follow the guidelines below to keep this information from being released by mistake.

- Keep client records (health and financial) and personal files in a locked room. You must sign out client records prior to use. Remember to also protect discharged charts.

- Only managers should have keys to the office or room. Keep track of the names of the people who have keys.

- Do not use boards to post patient information. Be sure computer screens do not face public areas

- Don't leave client information on your desk where others can see it when you are gone.

- When taking information to a doctor's office, put it in an envelope. Do not put the client's name or any information that would tell you who the client is on the envelope.

- Keep field charts in envelopes of containers.

- Be sure to destroy all copies of information that is not needed. **Shredding** is a great way to destroy unneeded information. Be sure you do not just throw away client information.

- When a client or the person paying the bill calls, ask the caller to give you 2-3 pieces of information only they would know. For example, date of birth, social security number or insurance ID. Tell the caller, "to protect your privacy, I'd like to ask a couple of questions." If the caller is not the client or the person paying the bill, make sure we have the client's permission to give the information to the caller. Take the caller's name and number so that you can call them back after you have checked for permission. This information is on the general consent.

- You can still discuss clients on your mobile telephone. If you are in an office and want to use the speaker phone to discuss client information, go into a room with a door.

- Watch where you are.  Do not talk about client information in a public place or when others are present.  If you are in a client's home and a guest is present, ask the client if it is okay to discuss his or her care with the guest.  When you are in the office, make sure that your conversation will not be heard by someone that is not a business associate ( a vendor, cleaning crew, mail person, family member of a coworker, etc.)
- When faxing information, be sure to use a cover sheet.  This sheet should have the company confidentiality statement.  Also verify the person's fax number and use speed dial.  You cannot receive a fax at a place of business that is not the company.  For example, you cannot receive a fax at your brother's restaurant down the street.

## Patient's Rights

Under the HIPPA rule, clients have several rights.  You must respond to all of these rights in a 30-60 day time frame so be sure to act on any requests as soon  they are received.

### Access

First, the client has the right to see his or her record.  This means the client can look at the record or get a copy or summary of the record.

If the request could hurt the client or someone else, the request can be refused.  If this happens, the client can ask again.  The client does not have the right to see information that was written in order to prepare for a law suit

The client can also request to get the record in a different location.  For example, if clients usually see their charts in an office, but the client is unable to leave home, the record should be brought to the client's home.

## Limitations

Clients are allowed to ask you to limit how you use protected information.  They cannot ask you to limit information that you send to them.  They can ask to limit information sent to other people.

You have the right to say no to the request if you think it is unfair.  For example, if a client's daughter is the main person providing care, she needs health formation in order to provide the care.  If the client asks you not to share information with the daughter, you can tell the client that you cannot provide care without giving the daughter information.

The client must ask for the limitation in writing.  If you agree to the limitation, you must follow it.  The only time you will not follow the limitation is when the client needs emergency care.  The limitation can be removed anytime the client changes his mind.

## Changes

The privacy rule also allows clients to change information in their records when they feel information is wrong.  This does not mean they can tear up or take out pages from our records. You can only change information to records that belong to you. If the client asks you to change items on records that you did not prepare, you cannot do so. For example, you cannot change information on hospital discharge summaries because these are prepared by hospitals. The client must ask to change information by writing it out. They also need to tell you what information is wrong.

You can tell the client that the record cannot be changed if:

- You did not create the information
- The information is not part of your record
- The information is not available to look at
- The information is accurate and complete


Clients can still disagree with you and write this down. It you give anyone their information in the future, you must include what the client wrote.

When you allow clients to change records, they can give you a list of who they want you to tell about the changes. You need to tell the people your client identifies about the changes. Changes should be written on a separate communication note. Do not write on the original document.

**Tracking Information That is Shared**

Information that you can share about the client is limited to what you need to provide care, collect payment and perform health care operations. The client is allowed to ask you who you have shared the information with.

Most of the time, you will have permission from the client to share information. There are times when information can be share without permission and tracking is not required. These include sharing information;

- With the client about his or her care
- With people involved in the client's care
- Required or permitted by law
- That occurred prior to April 14, 2003

Tracking must include the following pieces of information:

- Everything shared during the last 3 years unless listed above
- The date it was shared
- The name and address of the person who received the information
- A brief description of the information shared
- The reason they were given the information

## Costs of Not Following the Rules

It is very important to follow the rules. If you break these rules, you can be fined up to 25,000. If you abuse health information on purpose, the fines increase to up to 250,000.  You can also be sent to jail for up to 10 years.  Fines can also be brought against companies.

Remember, if your specific state has more strict laws, you must follow those instead.

## Reporting Abuse

If you think a client's rights have been abused, call the hotline to report the issue as well as discuss the issue with your manager.  The phone number is 888-9-NOTIFY.  You also need to choose a privacy officer.

## Summary

This workbook addresses how you can and cannot use or share client information.  It also covered protecting information from accidental sharing.  The client's rights have been listed as well as what can happen if you abuse information.

# CHAPTER 10

# SENIOR CARE COMPANY

# EMPLOYEE & POLICY MANUAL

## MISSION STATEMENT

Our mission is to help our client's maintain a clean, safe, and healthy living environment while living in the setting of their choice.

We pledge that we will:

- Develop a comprehensive plan to meet the client's wishes, abilities and directives as the central theme
- Provide trained professionals to implement the client's individualized plan
- Complete all jobs in a timely and efficient manner
- Promote quality, integrity, and respect for each client as we meet their needs

## Employment Policies

## Employment

(Your Company Name) strives to employ the most qualified individuals for all positions within the organization and to provide equal opportunities, see below. For all professional positions, (Your Company Name) will employ only individuals who meet the licensure or certification requirements for the particular professional position and are in good standing within the State Licensing Agency. (Your Company Name) will hire and develop employees basing judgment solely on job related qualifications.

## Staffing

Part-time and on-call personnel may be utilized in instances when the type of work, working schedule, and duration of employment permit.

## Minors

State and Federal legislation imposes certain limitations on the employment of persons under the age of 18. Therefore, applicants shall be required to furnish proof of age after an offer of employment has been made. Offers of employment shall be automatically revoked when applicants under 18 are not able to provide a work permit.

## Interviews

Pre-employment interviews are required for all positions. Interviews may be scheduled according to company needs.

## Tests

Written skills tests and competency testing may be administered to any employee.

# Health Screening & Immunization

Health Screening is required by all employees for TB testing (refer to Health Screening Policy).

## Employment at Will

The management of (Your Company Name) reserves the right to terminate the employment of any employee for any reason with or without cause and with or without notice at any time and recognizes the employee's right to the same. No employment, contracts, expressed or implied, exists in this company.

## Equal Opportunity Employer

It is (Your Company Name) policy to provide equal employment opportunity for qualified applicants without regard to race, color, religion, sex, age, marital status, national origin, or non-job related disability.

## Americans with Disabilities Act

(Your Company Name) shall not discriminate against a qualified individual with a disability because of the disability of such individual in regard to job application procedures, the hiring, advancements, or discharge of employees, employee compensation, job training, and other terms, conditions, and privileges of employment. Any employee who believes they are the victims of discrimination should report it immediately to their supervisor, to the owner, to the compliance hotline 800-496-5993.

### New Employees

All new employees must furnish a complete employment application including a valid social security number before starting work. They must also satisfy the federal rules for "Employment Eligibility Verification" by furnishing the required identification. No paycheck will be issued until all paper work is completed and all required information is furnished.

### Health Requirements

State law requires all new employees to have a pre-employment health screening to protect the clients against communicable diseases.

# Orientation

### Orientation Period

All new employees must complete a three-month orientation period. During this time you are closely supervised and observed to determine if you are responsible,

reliable and productive. A performance review may be initiated any time during this period and will always be completed at the end of this period to determine our suitability and eligibility of continued employment. If you are not recommended for continued employment at any time during the orientation period, you may be terminated immediately, without warning, for any reason deemed valid by the management.

If you are not recommended for continued employment at the end of this period you may also be terminated, or the orientation period may be extended, at the discretion of the management. If you are recommended for continued employment, you will become eligible for company benefits as defined in the employee benefits section and may be given merit raise based on the performance review.

## Uniforms and Dress Code

All employees are required to dress and groom in accordance with professional standards for their position. Homemakers and Personal Care employees are required to wear company scrubs and white tennis shoes, no open toes. The company will supply up to 3 sets of scrubs. The employee is responsible for any additional scrubs.

Maintenance/yard employees are required to wear a hat, shirt, blue or tan pants or shorts, and enclosed shoes.

### Gratuities, Gifts, Tips

The following guidelines are for all staff in regards to the acceptance of gifts, gratuities, tips, etc.

- Staff is strictly prohibited from asking a client for gifts, gratuities, tips, etc., or from any statement or request that could be interpreted as asking for something or expecting something.

- Clients have the right to give staff personal gifts if it is the residents' idea and personal choice to do so. However, the acceptance of any gift needs to be reviewed and approved by your supervisor for your own protection.
- Any gift of money must be declined or turned in to the employer.
- Contracts and/or agreements between client and staff outside of employment are discouraged and are to be fully disclosed to management for review of potential conflict of interest.
- Be careful and use common sense. Anything that may be construed to be coercion or conflict of interest could result in disciplinary action, loss of employment, or even prosecution.

# Time Sheets

## Time Sheets

(Your Company Name) business hours are 8:00 a.m. to 5:00 p.m. each weekly employee is expected to work during that time. Any job started must be finished.

Every Monday the client check list sheet and time sheets must be turned in. They also must be turned in by the 15th and last day of the month for pay roll.

## Attendance and Punctuality

When an employee is sick or has an emergency, it's the employee's responsibility to notify their supervisor and/or the office as soon as possible.

A doctor's note is required to be submitted to the supervisor upon returning to work. Failure to report to work without advanced notice, valid reason, or in case of sickness without a doctor's note is assumed to be your resignation without notice.

# Wages, Pay Raises, and Paydays

## Starting Pay

Each position has a minimum (and generally a maximum) wage that is determined by the company management. The starting pay may be higher than the minimum if the employee is experienced or has special qualifications. The wage ranges are based upon such factors as level of professional expertise, education required and market conditions. These wage ranges are adjusted annually to reflect changing conditions such as inflation increased reimbursement levels, or changing market conditions.

## Pay Raises

Pay raises may be given at the end of the orientation period, annually, when changes occur in the pay scales or when you are promoted. These raises are based upon the performance review.

The wage and the amount of pay raises are confidential information and should not be discussed with other employees, the clients, etc. If an employee feels there is a problem with the pay, it should be discussed with supervisor.

## Payday and Paychecks

Payday is the 24nd and 9th of the month. The payroll is calculated from the 1st to the 17th and 18th to end of month.

The company assumes no responsibility for time cards submitted by the employee that are incorrect. If paycheck is not correct see supervisor.

# Employee Benefits

## Eligibility for Benefits

Full time employees become eligible for employee benefits upon completion of the orientation period.

## Paid Time Off

(eligible after one year of employment with company)
Fourteen (14) days for full time employees (full time employees work 32 hours a week or more) will be paid a year. Paid holidays are included in these fourteen days, (Your Company Name) observes six paid holidays: New Year's, Memorial Day, Independence Day (July 4th), Labor Day, Thanksgiving Day and Christmas Day. These holidays are included in your fourteen (14) Paid Time Off days. If you choose to take the day off please assist the office in rescheduling your clients. If you work the

holidays you are paid double time or you can take another day off.

## Social Security

It is the responsibility of every employee to know about social security and every paycheck shows this deduction. The company matches your social security taxes and pays the entire amount into the social security trust fund on the employee's behalf.  This benefit costs the company in excess of 7.5% of employee's wages and helps provide the peace of mind all enjoy because social security is always there if and when you need it.

## Unemployment Compensation

The company pays a tax to both federal and state agencies to help insure that you have a "safety net" to rely on if you become unemployed and meet the criteria for unemployment compensation that is set by law.

## Workers Compensation Insurance

(Your Company Name) also provides Worker's Compensation Insurance so if an employee is injured on the job, medical bills will be covered.  If an employee should suffer a disabling injury on the job and is deemed unable to work, the fund protects the employee.

# Leave of Absence

## Granting Leave under Family Medical Leave Act

In accordance with the Family Medical Leave Act (FMLA) of 1993, employees who have worked for the company for the least one year or 1250 hours and are currently working 24 hours per week or more will be granted up to 12 weeks of <u>unpaid,</u> job protected leave of absence for any of the following reasons:

- To care for the employee's child after birth, or placement for adoption or foster care
- To care for employees spouse, child or parent who has a serious health condition
- For a serious health condition that makes the employee unable to perform the job

The employee must make written request to the owner for such leave on the form provided and ordinarily must give 30 days' advance notice when the leave is foreseeable. The employee may also be required to provide medical certification to support a request for leave for a serious health condition and/or fitness for duty report to return to work. All necessary forms are available at the administration office. Failure to comply with these requirements may result in denial of the request for leave.

Employees designated as "key employee" as defined in the Family medical Leave Act, may not be reinstated to an equivalent job with equivalent pay.

## Returning to Work

Upon return from FMLA approved leave, most employees will be restored to their original or equivalent position, with equivalent pay, benefits, and other employee terms.

## Non-FMLA Leave

Leave of absence for non-FMLA covered reasons must also be requested in writing on the form provided and will be granted solely at the discretion of the owner.  If granted, the terms of such leave (including length of leave, employee benefits, returning to work, job protection, etc.) will be worked out in advance and stated in writing by the owner and signed by the employee prior to approval.

# Employee Right and Responsibilities

## Sexual Harassment or Discrimination

The owner of (Your Company Name) will not tolerate sexual harassment or discrimination in any form. Any employee who believes they are the victim of sexual harassment or discrimination should report it immediately to their supervisor, to the owner, to the compliance hotline 800-496-5993 and may do so without fear of reprisal or ridicule.

All reported cases would be investigated thoroughly by the person receiving the report and then referred to the company owner, who will determine an appropriate course of action and inform the employee involved of the final outcome of the complaint.

Any employee who the management believes to be guilty of sexual harassment, discrimination or any other form of harassment (racial, color, religion, sex, national origin) will be subject to immediate termination without warning and loss of all benefits.

### Fair Treatment

The purpose of this employee handbook is to help insure that all employees are treated fairly and consistently. If any employee feels that they have not been treated fairly, the problem should be discussed with the supervisor. If this does not resolve the problem and the employee still feels they are not being treated fairly, follow the grievance procedure as outlined.

## Grievances or Complaints

Complaints or grievances that cannot be resolved through supervisor can be taken to owner. The owner will make every effort to be fair and will take whatever action is appropriate.

## Suggestion of Improvement

Suggestions on how to improve our services and programs are always welcome and should be directed to your supervisor or owner as circumstances dictate.Incidents or Injuries

Any employee injured on the job must report immediately to supervisor or owner. Worker's Compensation is available, but may be forfeited if the injury is not promptly and properly reported so that the appropriate documents can be filed. Claim forms must be filled out in a timely fashion to ensure proper coverage.

## Standards of Conduct/ Code of Ethics

Our goal and our purpose at (Your Company Name) are to provide each client with the finest quality of service available anywhere. Each employee is expected to treat all clients as well as other staff members, with respect and dignity and must maintain a professional standard of conduct at all times.

Employees are never permitted to;

Use a client's car without authorization

Consume a client's food or beverages

Consume alcohol immediately prior to or during a client visit

Use a client's phone for personal use

Discuss personal problems, religious, or political beliefs

Accept gifts or tips

Solicit or Accept money or goods or purchase items from clients

Bring another individual into a client's home

Smoke in a client's home

Breach a client's privacy or confidentiality

Assume control of a client's finances

Assume control of a client's personal affairs

Cooperation and courtesy among staff members is essential to quality service and is required of each employee.

## Other Policies

## Company Property

Any employee who is suspected or in any way misusing company property will be subject to termination, even if no conclusive **proof** exists of that employee's guilt. Possession of firearms or other weapons on company property is prohibited.

## Background Checks

Upon hire, all employees must submit to a mandatory background check. Failure to do so will result in denial of employment. If a criminal history exists, the employee must note that on the Employment Application and provide complete detail regarding that history. This includes all police reports, court records and probation/parole officer reports for each arrest and/or conviction. If a criminal history exists, the owner will determine whether or not offer of employment will be made.

## Reference check

Information supplied on the application form or during an interview will be subject to verification. Reference checks shall be made by (Your Company Name) and may be conducted by phone or mail.

## License Certification

For professional positions, all applicants must be able to furnish for inspection their current license or certificate. A copy of the applicant's original license or certificate shall be retained for the employment file. The agency shall obtain copies of updated license on an ongoing basis.

# Termination, Warnings and Disciplinary Action

## Voluntary Termination

When an employee resigns, two weeks' notice must be given in order to allow the supervisor time to find and train a replacement.

## Involuntary Termination

When a supervisor determines that termination should occur, the following steps will take place:

- The supervisor will suspend the employee immediately and recommend termination to owner.
- The owner will conduct a thorough review of both sides of the issue, including hearing the suspended employee's own story, if appropriate.
- The owner will then make a decision, document it, and report it to the suspended employee and supervisor.  No one but owner can terminate and employee.
- If the terminated employee is convinced the decision was unfair, the employee may contact owner and explain reasons. The owner will review the case for final decision and notify the employee.

### Warning and Disciplinary Action

When a supervisor determines disciplinary action is necessary or that an employee is performing unsatisfactorily, or that policy violations have occurred, a written warning may be issued to the employee.

This warning will be discussed with the employee and placed in the employee's file.  Failure to respond satisfactorily to such warning will result in additional disciplinary action, suspension or termination.

# Rights of the Management

### Employment at Will

The management of (Your Company Name) reserves the right to terminate the employment of any employee for any reason, with or without cause and with or without notice at any time and recognizes the employee's rights to the same.  No employment contracts, either expressed or implied, exist in this company.

I have read (Your Company Name) Employee Manual and agree to all terms and conditions.

_____

Employee Signature                                                    Date

# EMPLOYEE PAPERWORK AND FORMS

## Sample Non-Disclosure and Non-Competition Agreement

In consideration of the ongoing association between (Your Company Name) and the undersigned employee (hereinafter "Employee"), the parties hereto have entered into this Non-Disclosure and Non-Competition Agreement.

WHEREAS, in the course of its business operations, (Your Company Name) provides its clients products and services which, by nature of the business, include trade secrets, confidential and proprietary information, and other matters deemed material or important enough to warrant protection; and

WHEREAS, Employee, by reason of his/her employment with (Your Company Name) and in the course of his/her duties, has access to said secrets and confidential information; and

WHEREAS, (Your Company Name) has trade secrets and other confidential and proprietary information, including, but not limited to, **PROCEDURES, CLIENT LISTS, AND PARTICULAR DESIRES OR NEEDS OF SUCH CLIENTS** to which Employee has access in the course of his/her duties as an Employee.

NOW, THEREFORE, in consideration of the premises contained herein, the parties agree as follows:

Employee shall not, either during the time of his/her employment with (Your Company Name) or at any time thereafter either directly or indirectly, communicate, disclose, reveal, or otherwise use for his/her own benefit or the benefit of any other person or entity, any trade secrets or other confidential or proprietary information obtained by Employee by virtue of his/her employment with (Your Company Name), in any manner whatsoever, any such information of any kind, nature, or description concerning any matters affecting or relating to the (Your Company Name) business, or in the business of any of its **CLIENTS OR PROSPECTIVE CLIENTS**, except as required in the course of his/her employment by (Your Company Name) or except as expressly authorized by (Your Company Name) in writing.

During any period of employment with (Your Company Name), and for two (2) years thereafter, Employee shall not, directly or indirectly, induce or influence, divert or take away, or attempt to divert or take away and, during the stated period following termination of employment, call upon or solicit, or attempt to call upon or solicit, any of the clients or patrons of (Your Company Name) including, but not limited to, those upon whom he/she was directly involved, or called upon, or catered to, or with whom became acquainted while engaged in the employment of the (Your Company Name) business. Further, Employee shall not make any use of the information described herein, or cause or attempt to cause any other person to use such information for purposes other than the business of (Your Company Name).

**(YOUR COMPANY NAME):**

By: _____


Dated: _____, 20_____


**EMPLOYEE:**

By: _____


Dated: _____, 20_____

## Employee TB Questionnaire

Employees who have had a significant reaction to the TB skin test need to complete the following questionnaire annually. In addition, any employee that has had a significant TB skin test may elect to receive antibiotic treatment, at no cost, which has been shown to reduce the likelihood that a person will develop an active case of tuberculosis. Any employee that believes they have been exposed to TB or becomes symptomatic must notify their supervisor immediately.

Name _____

Yes  No

___  ___  I have experienced a new onset of **Fever**

___  ___  I have experienced a new onset of **Weakness**

___  ___  I have experienced a new onset of **Weight Loss**

___  ___  I have experienced a new onset of **Night Sweats**

___  ___  I have experienced a new onset of **Low-grade Fever**

___  ___  I have experienced a new onset of **Productive Cough**

Employee's Name:

   ___ ___ I have

had **Occasional**

**Coughing of Blood**

DATE OF HIRE:


   ___ ___ I have

had **Chest Pain**


Employee Signature _____

Date_____


- If employee answered yes to any of the above schedule a chest x-ray


- X-ray date _____

TB Skin: baseline

_____

Annual                              Result: ***

_____

Annual

_____

Annual

_____

Annual

_____

_____

_____

_____

\*\*\*

Chest x-ray: baseline

_____

                                  Result:

_____

Annual                    Result:

_____

Annual

_____

Annual

_____

Annual

_____

_____

_____

_____

_____

_____

_____

Date: _____

I, _____ agree that the _____vacuum
that I have been

        (print name

_____

Employee Signature

_____

Supervisor Signature

**Elder Abuse Quiz**

**Name _____**

1. In your own words define elder abuse

_____

_____

_____

2.    Which of the following are considered elder abuse?

      A.      Neglect

      B.      Physical Abuse

      C.      Financial Exploitation

      D.      All of the above

3.    ☐ True    ☐ False

Elder abuse is very common and most cases of such are reported.

4.    Which of the following is most likely to be a victim of abuse?

      A.      Female

      B.      Over the age of 75

      C.      Disabled

      D.      All of the above

5.    List 3 factors that might cause someone to become and abuser. _____

_____

_____

6.      ☐ True ☐ False

The elderly are more likely to be abused by a stranger than by a

family member.

7.      List 3 factors that indicate abuse may have occurred.

_____

_____

_____

8.      If you suspect abuse has occurred you should **not**

a.   Call your supervisor

b.   Let your client know they will not be punished for

reporting the abuse

c.   Confront the suspected abuser

d.   Follow up with your supervisor in a few days

9.   ☐ True      ☐ False

An overly protective or defensive caretaker is a sign there may be abuse going on in the home.

I have read and understand the training materials about **elder abuse.** I have completed and passed this comprehensive quiz. All incorrect answers were corrected and discussed with me.

_____                          _____

Employee Signature                                    Date

_____          ____

Instructor Signature                                    Date

## HIPAA Test

Name _____

1. List 3 examples of protected information

_____

_____

_____

2.    When do you need to protect a client's name, address and payment form?

       E.    When they are a Medicaid client

       F.    When an audit is expected

       G.    To notify the billing department

       H.    All of the above

3.  ☐ True      ☐ False

It is OK to talk about a client's diagnosis at lunch since the other employees also know the client.

4.    ☐ True     ☐ False

It is OK to discuss types of client diagnoses a person may see as part of developing their business.

5.    Which of the following is not protecting a client's information?

       A.    Giving only the information necessary to the employee

       B.    Giving only billing information to the billing department

       C.    Sending information by e-mail

D. Keeping client files in a locked filing cabinet

6. ☐ True  ☐ False

A signed contract with a client authorizes you to have access to their protected information.

7. Which of the following would <u>not</u> be a proper way to protect patient information?

E. Keep files locked.

F. Use patient boards to post information.

G. Shred all unneeded information.

H. Put patient files in envelope when transporting information.

8. List 2 ways that protected information could be released.

1.___  _____

___

2._____

___

9.  ☐ True ☐ False

A patient has the right to see his own record under any circumstances.

10.    Patient information can be shared without permission or tracking, <u>except</u>

      A.      With the patient about his own care

      B.      With the neighbor.

      C.      When required or permitted by law.

      D.      With situations before April 14, 2003.

11.    What is the fine for not following the HIPAA rules and regulations?

_____

_____

I have read and understand the training materials about **HIPAA.** I have completed and passed this comprehensive quiz.  All incorrect answers were corrected and discussed with me.

_____

_____

Employee Signature                    Date


_____

_____

Instructor Signature                   Date



**Employee Orientation**



Employee Name:_____ Hire Date:

_____

| TOPICS | Date | Employee | Supervisor |
|--------|------|----------|------------|
|        |      |          |            |

|  |  | Signature |  |
| --- | --- | --- | --- |
| Facility / Company Orientation |  |  |  |
| Job Description |  |  |  |
| Time Sheet |  |  |  |
| Sick, Vacation, Holiday, Scheduling time off |  |  |  |
| Employee Policy & Procedure Manual |  |  |  |
| Occurrence / Accident Reports |  |  |  |
| Dress Code |  |  |  |
| Performance Evaluation |  |  |  |
| Ordering Equipment / Supplies |  |  |  |
| Telephone Usage |  |  |  |
| Body Mechanics |  |  |  |
| Check Request |  |  |  |
| Credit Cards |  |  |  |
| Department Meetings / In-services |  |  |  |
| Documentation / Forms |  |  |  |
| Billing |  |  |  |
| Use / Maintenance of Equipment |  |  |  |
| Infection Control |  |  |  |
| Elder Abuse |  |  |  |

| | | |
|---|---|---|
| DMV Motor Vehicle Record | | |
| | | |
| Food Handler's Permit | | |
| CPR | | |

| | |
|---|---|
| | **Customer Service / Client Satisfaction** |
| | **Attention to detail** |
| | **On time** |
| | **Works additional hours, when necessary** |
| | **Neat, professional appearance** |
| | **Performs work with little, or no supervision** |
| | **Other.  Explain -** |

Employee needs continued or additional training in these areas:

| | |
|---|---|
| | Elder Abuse |
| | Cleaning standards |
| | Employee safety |
| | HIPAA privacy |
| | Personal care |
| | CPR |
| | Equipment maintenance |
| | Homemaking services |
| | Yard Care |
| | Maintenance |
| | Software training   circle one<br><br>QuickBooks      Scheduling Program      MS Word      MS Excel |

Employee's comments and/or opinions about work:

_____

_____

_____

_____

Employee's goals:

Long Term:

_____

_____

_____

_____

(To be completed by ____/____/____)

Short Term:

_____

_____

_____

_____

(To be completed by ____/____/____)

Owner/manager's review of employee's progress while working at (Your Company Name):

_____

_____

_____

_____

_____

_____

Action taken:

Wage:          Increase          [  ]          Position:

Improved          [  ]

Stays same          [  ]

Stays same          [  ]

Decrease          [  ]

Decrease          [  ]

Signed by employee to verify accuracy:

_____          _____

_____

Employee                                                        Owner/Manager


## Separation Notice -- Resignation


TO:            _____

               Owner/Operator


FROM:  _____

               Employee Name (please print)


               _____

               (Your Company Name) #

RE:        TERMINATION

This is to advise the management of (Your Company Name) that I am resigning my position because:

_____

_____

_____

_____

_____

_____

Effective date: _____, 20\_\_\_\_

**Separation Notice -- Termination**

**For Office Use Only:**

From: _____

        Owner/Operator (please print)

_____ has resigned/been terminated and I would like to make these additional comments:

_____

_____

_____

_____

_____

_____

                          Rehire? Yes [ ] No [ ]

Signature: _____ Date: _____, 20___

**Owner/Operator**

Signature: _____ Date:

_____, 20___

**Employee**

# CHAPTER 11

## Employee Training Materials

Aging changes quiz

Aging 2 quiz

Balance quiz

Bathing Grooming quiz

Body Mechanics quiz

Blood Pathogens quiz

Bowel and Bladder quiz

Communication quiz

Covered services quiz

Elder Abuse quiz

Fire Safety quiz

Food Safety quiz

Infection Control Quiz

Nutrition quiz

Poison Safety quiz

Skin Care quiz

3500 quiz

# AGING CHANGES QUIZ

Name _____

1.       What is the purpose of epithelial tissue?  CIRCLE ANSWER

        A.       To provide a frame for, and give shape to,
                 the body

        B.       To connect other types of tissue together

        C.       To cover the body and line its cavities

        D.       To conduct nerve impulses

2.               ☐ True          ☐ False

        The nervous system receives, processes and stores
        information

3.       Which of the following is a normal age-related change
         affecting the Integumentary system?  CIRCLE ANSWER

        A.       Nails become thick and tough

        B.       The body produces less sweat

        C.       The skin becomes dry and fragile

        D.       All of the above

4.      Which of the following is a function of the skeletal system? CIRCLE ANSWER

    A.    It acts as a storage site for vitamin C
    B.    It produces heat
    C.    It produces blood cells
    D.    All of the above

9.      When a muscle atrophies, it becomes: CIRCLE ANSWER

    A.    Larger and stronger
    B.    Thinner and weaker
    C.    Stiff
    D.    More flexible

10.     What part of the respiratory tract is also known as the "windpipe"? CIRCLE ANSWER

    A.    Pharynx
    B.    Epiglottis
    C.    Larynx
    D.    Trachea

11.     How does aging affect the nervous system?  CIRCLE ANSWER

A. Older people usually become "senile" and forgetful

B. Older people lose the ability to form or understand words

C. Older people may take slightly longer to react to things

D. Aging does not affect the nervous system because old neurons are constantly replaced

12. Hormones are chemical messengers that allow the body to: CIRCLE ANSWER

A. Metabolize energy

B. Grow

C. Reproduce

D. All of the above

13. Normal changes in the digestive system related to aging include: CIRCLE ANSWER

A. More difficulty chewing and swallowing

B. Sharper sense of taste and increased appetite

C. Decreased risk for constipation

D. All of the above

14. How does aging affect the urinary system? CIRCLE ANSWER

    A. The kidneys' ability to filter waste from the blood decreases

    B. The bladder is able to hold more urine

    C. The person's risk for constipation is increased

    D. The person's urine becomes darker

BODY MECHANICS QUIZ


Name _____


1.      What are three risk factors that lead to falls?


      _____

      _____


      _____


2.      Which one of the following does not give feedback to the brain about the position of the body?

    A.   Eyes

    B.   Joints, tendons, muscles

    C.   Kidneys

    D.   Ears

3. ☐ True  ☐ False

Falls are the leading cause of injury related death in the elderly.

4. Which of the following is not an accurate statistic?
CIRCLE ANSWER

        E. 30 – 40% of people over the age of 65 fall each year

        F. Multiple risk factors increase a person's risk of falling

        G. Women fall more often than men

        H. Pets are the most common cause of falls

5. ☐ True  ☐ False

When lifting, remember to use the large muscles of your hips and thighs.

6. Which of the following may help a person keep their balance?  CIRCLE ANSWER

        A. Good lighting

        B. Clean glasses

C.A grab bar

D.     All of the above

7.     ☐ True     ☐ False

Having a cold can increase an older person's risk of falls.

8.     ☐ True     ☐ False

If someone looses their balance you should do whatever you can to prevent a fall.

# ANSWER SHEET

1. Weakness, problems with walking, medications, slippery surfaces, poor lighting, loose rugs, obstacles (clutter)
2. C
3. True

4. D

5. True

6. D

7. True

8. False

## BATHING, GROOMING & MOBILITY QUIZ

Name _____

1. ☐ True ☐ False

   Range of Motion can improve blood flow to the skin and reduce chance of skin breakdown

2. ☐ True ☐ False

   It is better to rub a client to dry the skin than it is to pat the skin dry

3. When moving and positioning people, you should: CIRCLE ANSWER

        I.      Avoid friction and shearing

        J.      Use good body mechanics

        K.     Use pillows and rolled towels to maintain the position

        L.      All of the above

4. ☐ True ☐ False

Sitting at the edge of the bed before walking is called dangling

5. A person in the prone position is lying on his: CIRCLE ANSWER

        A.    Right side

        B.    Left side

        C.    Abdomen

        D.    Back

6. A nurse asks you to place a patient in the semi-Fowler's position while his tube feeding is running. You know the bed should be elevated: CIRCLE ANSWER

        A.   90 degrees

B. 60 degrees

C. 30 degrees

D. 15 degrees

7. ☐ True ☐ False

If client is not conscious do not talk to them during personal care activities

8. Why do you line the sink with a washcloth when cleaning a person's dentures? CIRCLE ANSWER

A. To have a washcloth handy

B. To protect the sink from scratches

C. To protect the dentures from breaking

D. To prevent contamination of the dentures

9. When giving a complete bed bath you should: CIRCLE ANSWER

A. Position yourself on one side of the bed and stay there

**B.** **Use the same water throughout the bath to minimize trips to the sink**

C. Avoid washing the person's perineal area because the person may be embarrassed

D. Keep the person covered as much as possible

10. ☐ True      ☐ False

Personal care provided whenever a person's condition warrants it is called, PRN

11. Which of the following observations make while assisting with oral care would you report to the nurse? CIRCLE ANSWER

A. Lips that are dry, cracked, swollen, or blistered

B. Irritations, sores, or white patches in the mouth or on the tongue

C. Bleeding, swelling, or redness of the gums

D. All of the above

BOWEL & BLADDER QUIZ

Name _____

1.    The most comfortable position for using a bedpan is:

CIRCLE ANSWER

      A.    Fowler's position

      B.    Sims' position

      C.    Prone position

      D.    Supine position

2.    In a person with a Foley catheter, why must the urine drainage bag be kept lower than the client's bladder?

CIRCLE ANSWER

      M.    Keeping the drainage bag below bladder level will prevent a bedridden person from seeing the bag, which he or she may find embarrassing

      N.    Keeping the drainage bag below bladder level will keep the client more comfortable in bed

      O.    Keeping the drainage bag below bladder level will prevent urine from returning to

the bladder, where it could cause
infection

P.      Keeping the drainage bag below bladder level will prevent the urine from leaking out

3.      Which one of the following describes normal urine? CIRCLE ANSWER

      A.      Cloudy with a strong odor

      B.      Well formed

      C.      Red-tinged

      D.      Clear, light yellow or golden with a slight odor

4.      When caring for a person who is incontinent of urine, it is important to: CIRCLE ANSWER

      A.      Provide good perineal care

      B.      Let the person know that his or her behavior is inappropriate, so it will stop

      C.      Take the person to the bathroom once daily

      D.      Restrict fluids to reduce the chance of an accident

5.      When caring for a person with an indwelling catheter, always remember to: CIRCLE ANSWER

        A.      Leave the drainage bag above the level of the bladder while the person is in bed

        B.      Tape any leaks at the connection site

        C.      Wear gloves when providing daily catheter care

        D.      Tape the drainage tube under the leg

6.      ☐ True     ☐ False

        Nocturia is when a client has blood in the urine

7.      A healthy person's feces will be: CIRCLE ANSWER

        A.      Black and tarry

        B.      Soft, brown, formed and moist with a distinct odor

        C.      Hard and pellet-like

        D.      Long and stringy

8.      To help your clients maintain healthy bowel function, it is important to: CIRCLE ANSWER

        A.      answer call lights promptly

B.     encourage them to eat a well-balanced

diet and drink

plenty of fluids

C.     assist them with exercise

D.     all of the above


9.     Your client has an ileostomy, and you assist him with

emptying his bag. What would you expect his feces to

be like? CIRCLE ANSWER

A.     very liquid

B.     hard, dry ,pellets

C.     soft, brown, moist, and formed

D.     none of the above


10.    When a person has a colostomy what part of the

intestine has been removed? CIRCLE ANSWER

A.     The Duodenum

B.     The Ileum

C.     The Jejunum

D.     The Colon

11.    Feces vary in consistency depending on what section of

the intestine was removed. If removed from near the

beginning of the intestine the stool will

be_____. If removed from near the end

of the colon the stools will

be_____.

12.     T or F An ostomy is an opening in the abdomen for the elimination of feces

13.     The passage of liquid, unformed feces is known as:

        A.     Fecal impaction

        B.     Constipation

        C.     Diarrhea

        D.     Fecal incontinence

# COMMUNICATION QUIZ

Name _____

1.      Which one of the following is an example of positive body language? CIRCLE ANSWER

        Q.      Nodding encouragingly as someone speaks

        R.      Crossing your arms across your chest

        S.      Tapping your feet or fingers

        T.      Rolling your eyes

2.      ☐ True        ☐ False

Grimacing when putting weight on a limb is an example of non-verbal communication

3.      An example of an action that blocks effective communication is: CIRCLE ANSWER

        E.      Interrupting

        F.      Not listening carefully

        G.      Being judgmental

H.      All of the above


4.      Which one of the following is an objective observation?
CIRCLE ANSWER

E.      "Mr. Wohl says that his back hurts when he coughs."

F.      "Ms. O'Connell's urine is cloudy, and has a strong odor"

G.      "Mr. McAndrews is complaining of a headache."

H.      "The resident in room 201B is complaining of a stomachache."


15.     Which one of the following is an example of nonverbal communication? CIRCLE ANSWER

E.      Using sign language to communicate with a deaf person

F.      Recording vital sign measurements in a patient's or resident's chart

G.      Gently touching a patient or resident on the shoulder to reassure her

H.      Making a telephone call

16.    What usually forms the basis for a subjective observation?
       CIRCLE ANSWER

                A.    A symptom or a patient or resident
                      complaint

                B.    A measurement

                C.    A doctor's order

                D.    All of the above

17.    When recording information in a person's chart, what
       should you remember to do? CIRCLE ANSWER

                A.    Use pencil so that errors can be corrected
                      easily

                B.    Sign, date, and time your entry

                C.    Update all of your client's information at
                      one time at the end of the day

                D.    All of the above

18.    What is it called when people have differences and they are
       unable to come to an agreement? CIRCLE ANSWER

                A.    Communication

                B.    Conflict

                C.    Culture

                D.    Personality differences

19. What should you do when a client is complaining of severe pain? CIRCLE ANSWER

    A. Try and find some pain medicine

    B. Go to the doctor and get some medicine

    C. Call your supervisor

    D. Ask a neighbor to borrow some pain medicine

20. Which of the following activities is a form of communication? CIRCLE ANSWER

    A. Telling someone something

    B. Giving a gift to someone

    C. Accepting a gift from someone

    D. Driving down to a friend's house to meet him

# Person Care Services QUIZ

Name _____

1.     Name three services that are covered by Medicaid

_____

_____

_____

_____

2. Name three services that are NOT covered by Medicaid

_____

_____

_____

_____

**Define the following Terms**

- Incapable caregiver

- Cueing

- Daily Record

- Instrumental Activities of Daily Living (IADLs)

- Personal Care Assistant (PCA)

# ELDER ABUSE QUIZ

Name _____

1. In your own words define elder abuse

   _____

   _____

   _____

2. Which of the following are considered elder abuse?

   a. Neglect

   b. Physical Abuse

   c. Financial Exploitation

   d. All of the above

3. 3. ☐ True   ☐ False

4. Elder abuse is more often reported than child abuse.

5. Which of the following is most likely to be a victim of abuse?

   i.   Female

   ii.  Over the age of 75

   iii. Disabled

        iv.   All of the above

6.        List 3 factors that might cause someone to become an abuser. _____

        a. _____

        b. _____

7.        ☐ True ☐ False

8.        The elderly are more likely to be abused by a stranger than by a family member.

9.        List 3 factors that indicate abuse may have occurred.

        a. _____

        b. _____

        c. _____

10.        If you suspect abuse has occurred you should **not**

        i.   Call your supervisor

        ii.   Let your client know they will not be punished for reporting the abuse

     iii.  Confront the suspected abuser

     iv.  Follow up with your supervisor in a few days

11.       9. ☐ True    ☐ False

12.       An overly protective or defensive caretaker is a sign there may be abuse going on in the home.

I have read and understand the training materials about **elder abuse.** I have completed and passed this comprehensive quiz. All incorrect answers were corrected and discussed with me.

_____

_____

Employee Signature                Date

_____

_____

Instructor Signature             Date

**FIRE SAFETY QUIZ**

Name _____

1.      Name the three elements that must be present for a fire to occur.

_____

_____

_____

2.      Name two items around a house that might be fuel for a fire.  MANY ANSWERS POSSIBLE

_____

_____

3.    ☐ True    ☐ False

Once a fire is started it no longer needs oxygen to keep burning.

4.    Which of the following is not a true statement?  CIRCLE ANSWER

      E.    Be familiar with your facility's fire safety policy.

      F.    Patients should not smoke around oxygen

      G.    It isn't necessary to know the locations of all the exits, your natural instinct to get to safety will kick in when a fire erupts.

      H.    Report any malfunctioning smoke detectors immediately.

5.    ☐ True    ☐ False

If you teach a child not to play with fire, you won't have to keep matches out of reach.

6.    When using a fire extinguisher, remember the word PASS. FILL IN THE MISSING WORD

**P**ull the _____ pin out.

**A**im the hose toward the _____ of the fire.

**S**queeze the _____.

**S**pray the contents of the fire _____ at the base of the fire using a _____          motion.

7.      Tell what the letters in the RACE fire response plan stand for.

R = _____

A = _____

C = _____

E = _____

8.    A type _____ is the most common type of fire extinguisher.

9.                  ☐ True    ☐ False

    The type ABC fire extinguisher can be used for all types of fires.

10.    What type of fire fueled by the item below cannot be put out with baking soda?

                A.    Gasoline

                B.    Cooking Oil

                C.    Electricity

                D.    Grease

11.  Match the type of extinguisher given in Column A, with the

        type of fire that it is used to extinguish, given in Column

B.

Column A ----        Column B ---

_____ Type A        A. Fire that is fueled by a petroleum product.

(e.g., gasoline, automotive oil, cooking oil, grease)

_____ Type B        B.    An electrical fire

C.    Fire that is fueled.

_____ Type C        (e.g., wood, paper, cloth, leaves, and grass)

12.        Write YES next to the type of fire that can be extinguished with water, and NO next to the type of fire that should not be extinguished with water.

Fire that is fueled by ordinary material such as wood, paper, cloth, leaves and grass.

_____ Fire that is fueled by petroleum products such as gasoline, cooking oil, grease

_____ An electrical fire

**ANSWERS**

1. FUEL, HEAT, OXYGEN

2. Cloth, Newspaper, Cooking Oil, Nail Polish, Bedding, Furniture, etc.

3. False – extinguishing the oxygen will put the fire out.

4. B –It isn't necessary to know the locations of all the exits, your natural instinct to get to safety will kick in when a fire erupts.

5. False –Don't tempt the child.

6. Pull the <u>SAFETY</u> pin out. Aim the hose toward the <u>BASE</u> of the fire.

   Squeeze the <u>HANDLE</u>. Spray the contents of the fire

   <u>EXTINGUISHER</u> at the base of the fire using a <u>SWEEPING</u> motion.

7. R = Remove    A = Activate    C = Contain    E = Extinguish or
Evacuate

8. ABC fire extinguisher

9. True

10. C -Electricity

11. <u>C</u> -Type A

   <u>A</u> -Type B

   <u>B</u> -Type C

12.    YES    - Fire that is fueled by ordinary material such as wood, paper, cloth, leaves and grass.

NO    - Fire that is fueled by petroleum products such as gasoline, cooking oil, grease.

NO    - An electrical fire.

**FOOD SAFETY QUIZ**

Name _____

1.    What is the single most important means of preventing the spread of disease through food?  CIRCLE ANSWER

I.    Buying only expensive food

J.    Cooking everything to well done

K.    Using only frozen food

L.    Hand washing by employees

2.    How do germs get in food?  CIRCLE ANSWER

E.    Poor hand washing after using the toilet

F.    They jump

G.     From one food to another (cross contamination)

H.     Both a and c

3.     How should you wash your hands?  CIRCLE ANSWER

E.     A quick rinse with cold water

F.     Use warm water and soap

G.     Scrub with warm water & soap for twenty seconds

H.     Scrub with hot water and sanitizer for one minute

4.     When should a food handler wash his/her hands?  CIRCLE ANSWER

A.     Between cutting a chicken and preparing a salad

B.     Before starting work

C.     Before smoking a cigarette

D.     Both a and b

5.     After washing, hands should be   CIRCLE ANSWER

A.      Dried with disposable towels

B.      Dried with a soft and clean cloth towel

C.      Allowed to air dry

D.      Wiped on your apron

6.      A food handler wears a uniform for the following reason:
CIRCLE ANSWER

A.      To protect against splattering food on your personal clothes

B.      To avoid contaminating food

C.      So that customers see that everyone works for the same company

D.      It is required by law

7.      What jewelry can you wear in a commercial kitchen?
CIRCLE ANSWER

A.      Anything

B.      Watches only

C.      Only a wedding ring

D.      Rings and bracelets if you wear gloves

8.      When should you wash your hands? CIRCLE ANSWER

A.     After touching raw meat

B.     After handling dirty dishes or kitchen equipment

C.     After sneezing, eating, or drinking

D.     All of the above

9.     Gloves should be: CIRCLE ANSWER

A.     Put on over washed hands

B.     Taken off carefully and reused

C.     Used for no more than 10 minutes at a time

D.     Turned inside out and reused

10     Sanitizers should be used: CIRCLE ANSWER

A.     Every time food is handled

B.     To clean with

C.     After surfaces are cleaned

D.     Never, they're dangerous

11     What is the difference between "clean" and "sanitary?" CIRCLE ANSWER

A.     None

B.   Clean means free of dirt; sanitary means free of germs

C.   If things are sanitary it means they are clean

D.   Both b and c

12.   Dish water needs to be changed: CIRCLE ANSWER

A.   Daily

B.   When it turns cold

C.   When it gets dirty

D.   Both b and c

13.   Pests need: CIRCLE ANSWER

A.   Food, water, a place to hide, warmth to breed

B.   Love and affection

C.   To be professionally exterminated

D.   Both a and c

14.   Surfaces should be   CIRCLE ANSWER

A.   Cleaned with a brush, soap & warm water, then rinsed and sanitized

B.   Wiped with a damp rag

C.   Cleaned with warm water and soap

D.        Sprayed with bleach

15.      Cross contamination means: CIRCLE ANSWER

A.        Germs passing from one food to another

B.        Food getting little cross-shaped marks all over it

C.        Germs from dirty equipment or kitchens getting into the food

D.        Both a and c

16.      Food can be cross contaminated by: CIRCLE ANSWER

A.        Other food

B.        Your hands

C.        Cooking utensils

D.        All of the above

17.      Thawing meats should be stored:  CIRCLE ANSWER

A.        On the top shelf of the refrigerator

B.        On the middle shelf of the refrigerator

C.        On the bottom shelf of the refrigerator

D.        Anywhere in the refrigerator

18.     Between cutting raw chicken and preparing salad on the same cutting board, the food handler should: CIRCLE ANSWER

    A.    Wipe off the knife and cutting board with a rag or sponge

    B.    Not do anything special since both foods are going to be eaten soon

    C.    Wash off the knife and cutting board with plain cold water

    D.    Wash off knife and cutting board with hot, soapy water and bleach

19.     If you take hamburgers off a plate with tongs to grill them, you should:  CIRCLE ANSWER

    A.    Use different tongs to take them off the grill

    B.    Put them on a different, clean, plate when they are cooked

    C.    Cook them to at least 155°F

    D.    All of the above

20.     Ingredients for a salad should be: CIRCLE ANSWER

    A.    Washed first

B.      Chilled first

C.      Left sitting at room temperature

D.      Both a and b

21.     The "Danger Zone" means: CIRCLE ANSWER

    A.      Temperatures where germs grow rapidly

    B.      Wet floors

    C.      Where food is most likely to become
            unsafe

    D.      All of the above

22.     The Danger Zone is: CIRCLE ANSWER

    A.      0°F to 70°F

    B.      40°F to 140°F

    C.      80°F to 110°F

    D.      140°F to 221°F

23.     "Out of temperature" means: CIRCLE ANSWER

    A.      Food that is frozen

    B.      Food that is so hot that it can burn a
            customer

    C.      Food that can't have its temperature take

D. Food that is in the Danger Zone for more than 2 hours

24. Can all the germs be killed?  CIRCLE ANSWER

    A. Yes, if we are very careful

    B. Yes, if all food is frozen first

    C. No, but we can keep them to a very small number

    D. No, they will grow no matter what we do

25. What foods do germs grow in best? CIRCLE ANSWER

    A. Moist foods

    B. High protein foods, like meat

    C. Foods low in acid, like vegetables

    D. All of the above

26. Germs can:  CIRCLE ANSWER

    A. Double their numbers every 20 minutes in the Danger Zone

    B. Survive freezing

    C. Survive being heated, and then start to grow again

D.      All of the above

25.     What foods do germs grow in best? CIRCLE ANSWER

      A.      Moist foods

      B.      High protein foods, like meat

      C.      Foods low in acid, like vegetables

26.     Hot foods should be cooled:  CIRCLE ANSWER

      A.      To 70F in two hours, then to 40F within 4 more hours

      B.      By dividing it into small pieces or into shallow pans

      C.      At room temperature

      D.      Both a and b

27.     The best way to cool a hot pot of soup is: CIRCLE ANSWER

      A.      Set the pot on the counter until it's cool, then place inside refrigerator

      B.      Set the pot, uncovered, inside the refrigerator

      C.      Set the pot in an ice bath, in a sink

D.     Let the pot sit on the turned off stove
       overnight to allow cooling

28.    Soup should be reheated:  CIRCLE ANSWER

A.     In the steam table at least an hour before
       serving
B.     On the stove top until it starts to steam
C.     On the stove top until it comes to a boil
D.     Never; reheated soup should never be
       served to the public

29.    You can determine if a chicken is cooked by: CIRCLE
ANSWER

A.     Looking at it
B.     Always cooking it the same length of time
C.     By touch to feel if its "springy"
D.     By sticking a thermometer into it

30.    About how many people a year get sick from food
poisoning? CIRCLE ANSWER

A.     A Few
B.     Hundreds
C.     Thousands
D.     Millions

31.    About how many people a year die from food poisoning?
CIRCLE ANSWER

A.    A Few

B.    Hundreds

C.    Thousands

D.    Millions


32.    Not washing hands after using the bathroom is:  CIRCLE
ANSWER

A.    Not a problem

B.    Disgusting

C.    A main cause of disease

D.    Both b and c


33.    When a food handler must taste food for proper
seasoning, he/she should... CIRCLE ANSWER

A.    Stick the tip of a pinky finger into the
       food, then lick the finger

B.    Use a spoon over and over just for that
       purpose

C.    Use a clean spoon only once

D.    Use the same disposable spoon as many
       times as needed

34.     Which of the following things are concerns in food safety? CIRCLE ANSWER

    A.    Cleanliness of counter tops
    B.    Open sores on employee's hands
    C.    Mice droppings on the kitchen floor
    D.    All of the above


35.     Minor cuts on the hands should be: CIRCLE ANSWER

    A.    Washed, bandaged, and covered by a clean glove
    B.    Washed only
    C.    Ignored
    D.    Referred to a hospital emergency room

# INFECTION CONTROL QUIZ

Name _____

1. Name 3 times when you should wash your hands:

   **Before performing a procedure**          **If hands are visibly soiled**

   **Before and after eating also after using restroom**

2. What is the most important way to reduce the risk of infection?
   **HAND WASHING**

3. You should wash your hands instead of using alcohol rub when hands are **visibly soiled**, contaminated with **Blood** or **Body fluid**, and when there is a buildup of emollients on hands.

4. <u>T</u> or F Alcohol rub is better for your skin than hand washing.

5. T or <u>F</u> it is not necessary to wash hands/apply alcohol rub after removing disposable gloves.

6. Universal precautions are a set of guidelines to protect you from **Bloodborne pathogens**.

7. When should gloves be worn?

   **When touching blood or body fluids which require universal precautions or non-intact skin**

   **Handling items or surfaces that are contaminated with blood or body fluids**

8. T or **F** When gloves are soiled there is no need to change them, just wipe them on your pants and continue what you are doing.

9. Name 3 signs of Staph Aureus

   **Redness**

   **Swollen**

   **Pus filled**

10. **T** or F TB is spread by coughing and sneezing of infected individuals

11. What is it called when some has the TB bacteria but they are not sick with TB disease?
    **Latent TB**

12. Who is most likely to develop TB disease from someone who has TB? **Family members** and **Care givers**

13. What organ does Hepatitis C affect? **Liver**

14. T or **F** Hepatitis C is always fatal

**NUTRITION QUIZ**

Name _____

3.      Which one of the following lists foods that are good sources of protein

         E.     steak, chicken, fish

         F.     spinach, carrots, beets

         G.     bread cereal, rice

         H.     Apples, bananas, oranges

4.      What is the single most important means of preventing the spread of disease through food?  CIRCLE ANSWER

         M.     Buying only expensive food

         N.     Cooking everything to well done

         O.     Using only frozen food

         P.     Hand washing by employees

3.      How do germs get in food?  CIRCLE ANSWER

         I.     Poor hand washing after using the toilet

         J.     They jump

K.      From one food to another (cross contamination)

L.      Both a and c

4.      Which of the following lists food that are good sources of carbohydrates?

E.      liver, fish, chicken

F.      Cereal, fruit, bread

G.      Milk, beans, cheese

H.      Water, soda, butter

5.      How should you wash your hands?  CIRCLE ANSWER

I.      A quick rinse with cold water

J.      Use warm water and soap

K.      Scrub with warm water & soap for twenty seconds

L.      Scrub with hot water and sanitizer for one minute

6.      When should a food handler wash his/her hands?  CIRCLE ANSWER

E.  Between cutting a chicken and preparing
    a salad

F.  Before starting work

G.  Before smoking a cigarette

H.  Both a and b


7.  After washing, hands should be   CIRCLE ANSWER

E.  Dried with disposable towels

F.  Dried with a soft and clean cloth towel

G.  Allowed to air dry

H.  Wiped on your apron


8.  A food handler wears a uniform for the following reason:
CIRCLE ANSWER

E.  To protect against splattering food on
    your personal clothes

F.  To avoid contaminating food

G.  So that customers see that everyone
    works for the same company

H.  It is required by law


9.  What jewelry can you wear in a commercial kitchen?
CIRCLE ANSWER

E.  Anything

F. Watches only

G. Only a wedding ring

H. Rings and bracelets if you wear gloves

10. When should you wash your hands? CIRCLE ANSWER

E. After touching raw meat

F. After handling dirty dishes or kitchen equipment

G. After sneezing, eating, or drinking

H. All of the above

11. Gloves should be: CIRCLE ANSWER

E. Put on over washed hands

F. Taken off carefully and reused

G. Used for no more than 10 minutes at a time

H. Turned inside out and reused

12. Sanitizers should be used: CIRCLE ANSWER

E. Every time food is handled

F. To clean with

G. After surfaces are cleaned

H. Never, they're dangerous

13.     What is the difference between "clean" and "sanitary?"
CIRCLE ANSWER

        E.     None

        F.     Clean means free of dirt; sanitary means free of germs

        G.     If things are sanitary it means they are clean

        H.     Both b and c


14.     Dish water needs to be changed: CIRCLE ANSWER

        E.     Daily

        F.     When it turns cold

        G.     When it gets dirty

        H.     Both b and c


15.     Pests need: CIRCLE ANSWER

        E.     Food, water, a place to hide, warmth to breed

        F.     Love and affection

        G.     To be professionally exterminated

        H.     Both a and c


16.     Surfaces should be   CIRCLE ANSWER

E.      Cleaned with a brush, soap & warm
        water, then rinsed and sanitized

F.      Wiped with a damp rag

G.      Cleaned with warm water and soap

H.      Sprayed with bleach


17.     Cross contamination means: CIRCLE ANSWER

        E.      Germs passing from one food to another

        F.      Food getting little cross-shaped marks all
                over it

        G.      Germs from dirty equipment or kitchens
                getting into the food

        H.      Both a and c


18.     Food can be cross contaminated by: CIRCLE ANSWER

        E.      Other food

        F.      Your hands

        G.      Cooking utensils

        H.      All of the above


19.     Thawing meats should be stored:  CIRCLE ANSWER

        E.      On the top shelf of the refrigerator

F.      On the middle shelf of the refrigerator

G.      On the bottom shelf of the refrigerator

H.      Anywhere in the refrigerator

20.      Between cutting raw chicken and preparing salad on the same cutting board, the food handler should: CIRCLE ANSWER

      E.      Wipe off the knife and cutting board with a rag or sponge

      F.      Not do anything special since both foods are going to be eaten soon

      G.      Wash off the knife and cutting board with plain cold water

      H.      Wash off knife and cutting board with hot, soapy water and bleach

21.      If you take hamburgers off a plate with tongs to grill them, you should:  CIRCLE ANSWER

      E.      Use different tongs to take them off the grill

      F.      Put them on a different, clean, plate when they are cooked

      G.      Cook them to at least 155°F

      H.      All of the above

22.     Ingredients for a salad should be: CIRCLE ANSWER

      E.     Washed first

      F.     Chilled first

      G.     Left sitting at room temperature

      H.     Both a and b

23.     The "Danger Zone" means: CIRCLE ANSWER

      E.     Temperatures where germs grow rapidly

      F.     Wet floors

      G.     Where food is most likely to become unsafe

      H.     Both A & C

24.     The Danger Zone is: CIRCLE ANSWER

      E.     0°F to 70°F

      F.     40°F to 140°F

      G.     80°F to 110°F

      H.     140°F to 221°F

25.     "Out of temperature" means: CIRCLE ANSWER

E.  Food that is frozen

F.  Food that is so hot that it can burn a
    customer

G.  Food that can't have its temperature take

H.  Food that is in the Danger Zone for more
    than 2 hours

26.  Can all the germs be killed?  CIRCLE ANSWER

E.  Yes, if we are very careful

F.  Yes, if all food is frozen first

G.  No, but we can keep them to a very small
    number

H.  No, they will grow no matter what we do

27.  What foods do germs grow in best? CIRCLE ANSWER

E.  Moist foods

F.  High protein foods, like meat

G.  Foods low in acid, like vegetables

H.  All of the above

28.  Germs can:  CIRCLE ANSWER

E.    Double their numbers every 20 minutes in the Danger Zone

F.    Survive freezing

G.    Survive being heated, and then start to grow again

H.    All of the above

29.    Cardiac diets reduce: CIRCLE ANSWER

D.    Moist foods

E.    carbohydrates

F.    Foods low in acid, like vegetables

G.    Fats and protein

30.    Hot foods should be cooled:  CIRCLE ANSWER

E.    To 70F in two hours, then to 40F within 4 more hours

F.    By dividing it into small pieces or into shallow pans

G.    At room temperature

H.    Both a and b

31.    The best way to cool a hot pot of soup is: CIRCLE ANSWER

E. Set the pot on the counter until it's cool, then place inside refrigerator

F. Set the pot, uncovered, inside the refrigerator

G. Set the pot in an ice bath, in a sink

H. Let the pot sit on the turned off stove overnight to allow cooling

32. Soup should be reheated:  CIRCLE ANSWER

E. In the steam table at least an hour before serving

F. On the stove top until it starts to steam

G. On the stove top until it comes to a boil

H. Never; reheated soup should never be served to the public

33. You can determine if a chicken is cooked by: CIRCLE ANSWER

E. Looking at it

F. Always cooking it the same length of time

G. By touch to feel if its "springy"

H. By sticking a thermometer into it

34. About how many people a year get sick from food

poisoning? CIRCLE ANSWER

   E.  A Few

   F.  Hundreds

   G.  Thousands

   H.  Millions

35.  About how many people a year die from food poisoning? CIRCLE ANSWER

   E.  A Few

   F.  Hundreds

   G.  Thousands

   H.  Millions

36.  Potassium is important in the diet because:  CIRCLE ANSWER

   E.  It increases longevity

   F.  It promotes a regular heart beat

   G.  It promotes regular muscle contractions

   H.  Both b and c

37.  When a food handler must taste food for proper seasoning, he/she should... CIRCLE ANSWER

E.  Stick the tip of a pinky finger into the food, then lick the finger

F.  Use a spoon over and over just for that purpose

G.  Use a clean spoon only once, then get a new spoon if needed

H.  Use the same disposable spoon as many times as needed


38.  Which of the following things are concerns in food safety? CIRCLE ANSWER

E.  Cleanliness of counter tops

F.  Open sores on employee's hands

G.  Mice droppings on the kitchen floor

H.  All of the above


39.  Minor cuts on the hands should be: CIRCLE ANSWER

E.  Washed, bandaged, and covered by a clean glove

F.  Washed only

G.  Ignored

H.  Referred to a hospital emergency room

## Poison Control

## http://www.cdc.gov/health/poisoning.html

Poisoning occurs when people drink, eat, breathe, inject, or touch enough of a chemical (poison) to cause illness or death. Some poisons in very small amounts can cause illness or injury. Injury or illness may occur very quickly after exposure or may take several years with long-term exposure. The Centers for Disease Control and Prevention (CDC) defines a poisoning that occurs by accident as "unintentional poisoning" and a poisoning that results from a conscious, willful decision (such as suicide or homicide) as "intentional poisoning." CDC is supporting efforts to track, investigate, and prevent poisonings.

## http://www.cdc.gov/ncipc/factsheets/poisonpreventio n.htm

Tips to Prevent Poisonings

Poison Control Number

**1-800-222-1222**

**Safety Tips for You, Your Family, and Friends**

Unless noted, the safety tips below were adapted from the American Association of Poison Control Centers' poison prevention tips for children and adults.

**Drugs and Medicines**

- Follow directions on the label when you give or take medicines. Read all warning labels. Some medicines cannot be taken safely when you take other medicines or drink alcohol.
- Turn on a light when you give or take medicines at night so that you know you have the correct amount of the right medicine.
- Keep medicines in their original bottles or containers.
- Never share or sell your prescription drugs.
- Keep opioid pain medications, such as methadone and oxycodone, in a safe place that can only be reached by people who take or give them.
- Monitor the use of medicines prescribed for children and teenagers, such as medicines for attention deficit disorder, or ADD (SAMHSA 2006).
- Be careful when you dispose of drugs that can be abused, such as opioid pain medication and psychotherapeutic drugs. Drug users may look in the trash for them. Ask your pharmacist if he or she can take back old or expired medicines as well as any that you don't need (EPA 2006).

## Household Chemicals and Carbon Monoxide

- Always read the label before using a product that may be poisonous.
- Turn on the fan and open windows when using chemical products such as household cleaners.
- Wear protective clothing (gloves, long sleeves, long pants, socks, shoes) if you spray pesticides or other chemicals.
- Never mix household products together. You can make a poisonous gas by mixing chemicals such as ammonia and bleach.
- Keep chemical products in their original bottles or containers. Do not use food containers such as cups, bottles, or jars to store chemical products such as cleaning solutions or beauty products.
- Read these carbon monoxide poisoning prevention guidelines.
- Put the poison control number, 1-800-222-1222, on or near every home telephone and save it on your cell phone. The line is open 24 hours a day, 7 days a week.

## What to do if a poisoning occurs

1. Remain calm
2. Call 911 if you have a poison emergency and the victim has collapsed or is not breathing. If the victim is awake and alert, dial 1-800-222-1222. Try to have this information ready:

- the victim's age and weight
- the container or bottle of the poison if available
- the time of the poison exposure
- the address where the poisoning occurred

3. Stay on the phone and follow the instructions from the emergency operator or poison control center.

# http://www.carbon-monoxide-poisoning.com/symptoms.html

## Carbon Monoxide Poisoning Symptoms

Because carbon monoxide is odorless and colorless it is not always evident when it has become a problem is the home. Often people who have a mild to moderate problem will find they feel sick while they spend time at home. They might feel a little better outside in the fresh air but will have re-occurring symptoms shortly after returning home. If other members of the family have re-occurring bouts with flu-like symptoms while fuel-burning appliances are being used it may be time to have the house checked by a professional.

## Carbon Monoxide Detectors

Besides having a professional come into your home to check your appliances a carbon monoxide detector can be used to keep a constant watch over the levels of carbon monoxide in the home throughout the year.

**Symptoms of Carbon Monoxide Poisoning**

Low levels of carbon monoxide poisoning can be confused with flu symptoms, food poisoning or other illnesses and can have a long term health risk if left unattended. Some of the symptoms are the following.

- Shortness of breath
- Mild nausea
- Mild headaches

Moderate levels of CO exposure can cause death if the following symptoms persist for a long measure of time.

- Headaches
- Dizziness
- Nausea
- Light-headedness

High levels of CO can be fatal causing death within minutes.

**Treatment Options**

There are immediate measures you can take to help those suffering from carbon monoxide poisoning.

- Get the victim into fresh air immediately.
- If you cannot get the people out of the house, then open all windows and doors. Any combustion appliances should be turned off.

- Take those who were subjected to carbon monoxide to a hospital emergency room as quickly as possible. A simple blood test will be able to determine if carbon monoxide poisoning has occurred.

**http://www.bt.cdc.gov/agent/chlorine/basics/facts.asp**

**Facts about Chlorine**

**What chlorine is**

- Chlorine is an element used in industry and found in some household products.
- Chlorine is sometimes in the form of a poisonous gas. Chlorine gas can be pressurized and cooled to change it into a liquid so that it can be shipped and stored. When liquid chlorine is released, it quickly turns into a gas that stays close to the ground and spreads rapidly.
- Chlorine gas can be recognized by its pungent, irritating odor, which is like the odor of bleach. The strong smell may provide an adequate warning to people that they have been exposed.
- Chlorine gas appears to be yellow-green in color.
- Chlorine itself is not flammable, but it can react explosively or form explosive compounds with other chemicals such as turpentine and ammonia.
- 
- Where chlorine is found and how it is used

- Chlorine was used during World War I as a choking (pulmonary) agent.
- Chlorine is one of the most commonly manufactured chemicals in the United States. Its most important use is as a bleach in the manufacture of paper and cloth, but it is also used to make pesticides (insect killers), rubber, and solvents.
- Chlorine is used in drinking water and swimming pool water to kill harmful bacteria. It is also as used as part of the sanitation process for industrial waste and sewage.
- Household chlorine bleach can release chlorine gas if it is mixed with other cleaning agents.

**How people can be exposed to chlorine**

- People's risk for exposure depends on how close they are to the place where the chlorine was released.
- If chlorine gas is released into the air, people may be exposed through skin contact or eye contact. They may also be exposed by breathing air that contains chlorine.
- If chlorine liquid is released into water, people may be exposed by touching or drinking water that contains chlorine.
- If chlorine liquid comes into contact with food, people may be exposed by eating the contaminated food.
- Chlorine gas is heavier than air, so it would settle in low-lying areas.

**How chlorine works**

- The extent of poisoning caused by chlorine depends on the amount of chlorine a person is exposed to, how the person was exposed, and the length of time of the exposure.
- When chlorine gas comes into contact with moist tissues such as the eyes, throat, and lungs, an acid is produced that can damage these tissues.

**What the long-term health effects are**

- Long-term complications from chlorine exposure are not found in people who survive a sudden exposure unless they suffer complications such as pneumonia during therapy. Chronic bronchitis may develop in people who develop pneumonia during therapy.

**How people can protect themselves, and what they should do if they are exposed to chlorine**

- Leave the area where the chlorine was released and get to fresh air. Quickly moving to an area where fresh air is available is highly effective in reducing exposure to chlorine.
  - If the chlorine release was outdoors, move away from the area where the chlorine was released. Go to the highest ground possible, because chlorine is heavier than air and will sink to low-lying areas.
  - If the chlorine release was indoors, get out of the building.

- If you think you may have been exposed, remove your clothing, rapidly wash your entire body with soap and water, and get medical care as quickly as possible.
- *Removing and disposing of clothing:*
  - Quickly take off clothing that has liquid chlorine on it. Any clothing that has to be pulled over the head should be cut off the body instead of pulled over the head. If possible, seal the clothing in a plastic bag. Then seal the first plastic bag in a second plastic bag. Removing and sealing the clothing in this way will help protect you and other people from any chemicals that might be on your clothes.
  - If you placed your clothes in plastic bags, inform either the local or state health department or emergency personnel upon their arrival. Do not handle the plastic bags.
  - If you are helping other people remove their clothing, try to avoid touching any contaminated areas, and remove the clothing as quickly as possible.
- *Washing the body:*
  - As quickly as possible, wash your entire body with large amounts of soap and water. Washing with soap and water will help protect people from any chemicals on their bodies.
  - If your eyes are burning or your vision is blurred, rinse your eyes with plain water for 10 to 15 minutes. If you

wear contacts, remove them before rinsing your eyes, and place them in the bags with the contaminated clothing. Do not put the contacts back in your eyes. You should dispose of them even if you do not wear disposable contacts. If you wear eyeglasses, wash them with soap and water. You can put the eyeglasses back on after you wash them.

- If you have ingested (swallowed) chlorine, do not induce vomiting or drink fluids.
- Seek medical attention right away. Dial 911 and explain what has happened.

**How chlorine exposure is treated**

No antidote exists for chlorine exposure. Treatment consists of removing the chlorine from the body as soon as possible and providing supportive medical care in a hospital setting.

## POISON SAFETY QUIZ

Name _____

1.       Name five ways poison can enter the body?

_____

_____

_____

_____

_____

2.       Always _____ the label before using a product that may be poisonous.

3.              ☐ True     ☐ False

Poison Control Number is 1-800-222-1222 and is open 9:00 to

5:00 Monday through Friday.

4.      Which of the following is not a true poison safety guideline?  CIRCLE ANSWER

        A.      Always read the label before using a product that may be poisonous

        B.      Turn on a fan or open a window when using chemical products such as household cleaners

        C.      Ammonia and bleach are versatile chemicals and can be safely mixed with most products

        D.      Keep chemical products in their original bottles or containers

5.              ☐ True         ☐ False

        Even if you memorize the poison control number you should have it written on or near every                    home phone and save it on your cell phone.

6.      What four questions do you need to be ready to answer when you call poison control?

_____

_____

_____

_____

7.　　　　☐ True　　　☐ False

Because carbon monoxide is odorless and colorless it is not always evident when it has become a　　　problem is the home.

8.　　Low levels of carbon monoxide poisoning can be confused with _____ _____.

9.　　Having a _____ _____ _____ in the home can help keep a constant watch　　　over the levels of carbon monoxide in the home throughout the year.

Unscramble words to find answer:  NOCRAB  XMOONDIE  COREDETT

10.     Moderate levels of CO exposure can cause death if the following symptoms persist for a long        measure of time.
FILL IN MISSING LETTERS

H _ A _ A _ _ E S  ■  _ _ Z _ I _ _ _ S

■

_ A _ S _ A  ■  _ _ G _ T – H E _ D _ _

_ E S _

11.     Which of the following is not a true statement about chlorine?  CIRCLE ANSWER

A.     Chlorine was used during World War I as a choking (pulmonary) agent

B. Chlorine is one of the most commonly manufactured chemicals in the U.S.

C. Chlorine is never used in drinking water, as it is poisonous in any amount

D. Household chlorine bleach can release chlorine gas if it is mixed with other cleaning agents

12. ☐ True ☐ False

Chlorine gas is heavier than air, so it would settle in low-lying areas

13. What kind of cleanser do you wash with if your skin has been exposed to chlorine?

_____ and _____.

14. Put an "X" next to the incorrect statement.

_____ If you have ingested (swallowed) chlorine, induce vomiting right away.

_____ If chlorine was released indoors, get out of

the building.

_____ No antidote exists for chlorine exposure.

**ANSWERS**

1. DRINK, EAT, BREATH, INJECT, OR TOUCH

2. Read

3. False – Phone number is true, but poison control is open 24 hrs a day 7 days a week.

4. C – Ammonia and bleach are versatile chemicals and can be safely mixed with most products

5. True – Most people forget phone numbers in an emergency.

6.  The victim's age and weight

    The container or bottle of the poison if available

    The time of the poison exposure

    The address where the poisoning occurred

7.  True

8.  Flu Symptoms

9.  CARBON MONOXIDE DETECTOR

10. HEADACHES ■ DIZZINESS ■ NAUSEA ■ LIGHT-HEADEDNESS

11. C –Chlorine is never used in drinking water, as it is poisonous in any amount

12. True

13.  Soap and water.


14.  <u>X</u>  - If you have ingested (swallowed) chlorine, induce vomiting right away.

## SKIN CARE QUIZ

Name _____

1.  ☐ True    ☐ False

    You should always use soap when bathing a client with a skin lesion

2.  An abrasion or wearing away of the top layer of the skin that is caused by trauma is called a/an:   CIRCLE ANSWER

    Q.    Excoriation

    R.    Fissure

    S.    Macule

    T.    Papule

3.  Putting a pillow under a clients arm is an example of a/an:   CIRCLE ANSWER

    A.    Supportive device

    B.    Assistive device

C.	Draw sheet

D.	Shearing device

4.	A deep crack in the skin is called a/an:  CIRCLE ANSWER

    A.	Excoriation

    B.	Fissure

    C.	Macule

    D.	Papule

5.	Where are pressure ulcers most likely to form?  CIRCLE ANSWER

    A.	On the heels, ankles, and toes

    B.	On the elbows, and shoulder blades

    C.	On the spine

    D.	All of the above

6.	What is the underlying cause of all pressure ulcers?  CIRCLE ANSWER

    A.	Continuous pressure applied to one area

    B.	Poor nutrition

    C.	Incontinence

    D.	All of the above

7.      Which of the following risk factors can increase a person's risk of getting a pressure ulcer?   CIRCLE ANSWER

   A.      Advanced age
   B.      Incontinence
   C.      Poor nutrition
   D.      All of the above


8.      If you have a client with limited mobility, what can you do to decrease your client's risk of developing a pressure ulcer?  CIRCLE ANSWER

   A.      Dry the clients skin thoroughly after each bath
   B.      Reposition client regularly, according to your care plan
   C.      Encourage the client to eat well
   D.      All of the above


9.      ☐ True     ☐ False

   If you see a reddened area you had not noticed before you should notify your supervisor


10.  ☐ True     ☐ False

Good nutrition is required for a wound to heal

**3500 QUIZ**

Name _____

1.          ☐ True     ☐ False

The goal of the Nevada Medicaid Personal Care Services (PCS) program is to assist, support, and maintain recipients living independently in their homes

2.          ☐ True     ☐ False

Personal care services may be provided by any willing and qualified provider once approved by the Division of Health Care Financing and Policy (DHCFP)

3.          ☐ True     ☐ False

Personal Care Services can be provided through the PCS

program to residents of a nursing home

**Define the following Terms**

4. Incapable caregiver

5. Cueing

6. Daily Record

7. Instrumental Activities of Daily Living (IADLs)

8. Personal Care Assistant (PCA)

9-11. Name three services that are covered by Medicaid

_____

_____

_____

_____

12-14.     Name three services that are NOT covered by Medicaid

_____

_____

_____

_____

15.     An adverse action refers to a change in services such as:
        CIRCLE ANSWER

                U.  Denial

                V.  Reduction

                W.  Termination

                X.  All of the above

16. Provider responsibility includes all of the following except: CIRCLE ANSWER

    A. Comply with local, state and federal regulations
    B. Provide qualified employees
    C. Reimburse legally responsible adults for providing care
    D. Provide only services listed under "covered services"

17. During the verification of compliance visit, the provider must present written policies and procedures for all of the following except: CIRCLE ANSWER

    A. Compliance with TB testing
    B. Compliance with giving clients injections of insulin
    C. Compliance with requirements for FBI criminal background checks
    D. Compliance with the provision of backup services

18-22. Match the term with the best description: CIRCLE ANSWER

24 hour accessibility

**A.** the provider must provide Nevada Medicaid written notification  of serious occurrences involving the recipient or PCA

Serious occurrences

**B.** Provider shall obtain prior authorization for services

Prior authorization

**C.** Providers shall indemnify, hold harmless and defend DHCFP from all liability, claims, actions, damages, expenses, etc

Quality assurance

**D.** Provider shall maintain twenty-four (24) hour, 7 day per week landline telephone contact availability

Provider liability

**E.** Provider shall conduct an annual recipient satisfaction survey and utilize results to improve services

23. Which of the following is included on the prior authorization form: CIRCLE ANSWER

    A. Dates of service
    B. Hours and time per day
    C. Number of days per week
    D. Total authorized units per billing cycle
    E. All of the above

24. This request is made when a client requires and extra visit for an unanticipated need: CIRCLE ANSWER

    A. Single-service Authorization Request
    B. Mileage Authorization Request

C. Reimbursement

D. All of the above

25.  ☐ True   ☐ False

Initial requests for assessments to initiate Personal Care Services can be made by a recipient, a legally responsible adult, personal care representative, or an individual covered under the confidentiality requirements of HIPAA, but not by the provider.

**3500 answers to  QUIZ**

1. True

2. True

3. False

4. A caregiver who is unable to safely manager required care

5. Any spoken instructions or physical guidance which serve as a signal to do something

6. The daily documentation completed by the PCA indicating the time spent and services provided

7. IADL's capture more complex life activities and include light housekeeping, laundry, meal preparation and grocery shopping

8. A PCA is an individual who provides assistance with ADLs or IADLs to recipients with disabilities and chronic conditions

9-14 See section 3503 page 1,2

15. D

16. C


17. B


18 – 22  D, A, B, E, C


23. E


24. A

# Notice of Privacy Practices

This Notice of Privacy Practices describes how (Your Company Name) may use and disclose your protected health information to carry out treatment, payment or healthcare operations and for other purposes that are permitted or required by law. It also describes your rights to access and control your protected health information. "Protected health information" is information about you, including demographic information, that may identify you and that relates to your past, present or future physical or mental health or condition and related healthcare services.

We understand that medical information about you and your health is personal. We are committed to protecting medical information about you. We are required to abide by the terms of this Notice of Privacy Practices. We may change the terms of our notice at any time. The new notice will be effective for all protected health information that we maintain at that time. Upon your request, you can receive any revised Notice of Privacy Practices by contacting the (Your Company Name) Office. Just request that a revised copy be sent to you in the mail or ask for one at your next visit.

**How We May Use and Disclose Your Protected Health Information**

Your protected health information may be used and disclosed by your healthcare provider, our office staff and others outside of our facility that are involved in your care and treatment for the purpose of providing healthcare services to you. Your protected health information may also be used and disclosed to pay your healthcare bills and to support the operation of (YOUR COMPANY NAME).

Following are examples of the types of uses and disclosures of your protected healthcare information that (YOUR COMPANY NAME) is permitted to make. These examples are not meant to be exhaustive, but to describe the types of uses and disclosures that may be made by our facility.

**Treatment:** We may use protected health information about you to provide you with medical treatment or services. We may disclose medical information about you to doctors, nurses, technicians, medical students or other personnel who are involved in your care. Different departments of our facility also may share protected health information about you in order to coordinate your needs, such as physician appointments. We also may disclose protected health information about you to individuals outside of (YOUR COMPANY NAME) who may be involved in your medical care, such as family members or others we use to provide services that are part of your care. When required, we will obtain your authorization before disclosing any of your information. Only the minimal amount of information will be revealed during any disclosures.

**Payment:** Your protected health information will be used, as needed, to obtain payment of your healthcare services. This may include certain activities that your health insurance plan may undertake before it approves or pays for the healthcare services we recommend for you such as; making a determination of eligibility or coverage for insurance benefits, reviewing services provided to you for medical necessity and undertaking utilization review activities.

**Healthcare Operations:** We may use or disclose as-needed, your protected health information in order to support the business activities of your healthcare provider and (YOUR COMPANY NAME). These activities include, but are not limited to, quality assessment activities, employee review activities, training of medical students, licensing, marketing and fundraising activities, and conducting or arranging for other business activities.

For example, your health information may be disclosed to members of the medical staff, risk or quality improvement personnel and others to:

• Evaluate the performance of our staff

• Assess the quality of care and outcomes in your case and similar cases

• Learn how to improve our facilities and services

• Determine how to continually improve the quality and effectiveness of the health care we provide

In addition, We may use or disclose your protected health information, as necessary, to contact you to remind you of your appointment.

We will share your protected health information with third party "business associates" that may perform various activities (e.g., billing, transcription services) for (YOUR COMPANY NAME). Whenever an arrangement between our facility and a business associate involves the use or disclosure of your protected health information, we will have a written contract that contains terms that will protect the privacy of your protected health information.

We may use or disclose your protected health information, as necessary, to provide you with information about treatment alternatives or other health-related benefits and services that may be of interest to you.

**Other Permitted and Required Uses and Disclosures That May Be Made With Your Authorization, or Opportunity to Object**

You have the opportunity to agree or object to the use or disclosure of all or part of your protected health information. If you are not present or able to agree or object to the use or disclosure of the protected health information, then your healthcare provider may, using professional judgment, determine whether the disclosure is in your best interest. In this case, only the protected health information that is relevant to your healthcare will be disclosed.  We may use and disclose your protected health information in the following instances.


**Facility Directories**: Unless you object, we will use and disclose in our facility directory your name, the location at which you are receiving care, and your condition (in general terms).  All of this information, will be disclosed to people that ask for you by name. Members of the clergy will be told of your religious affiliation. Others Involved in Your

Healthcare: Unless you object, we may disclose to a member of your family, a relative, a close friend or any other person you identify, your protected health information that directly relates to that person's involvement in your healthcare. If you are unable to agree or object to such a disclosure, we may disclose such information as necessary if we determine that it is in your best interest based on our professional judgment.  We may use or disclose protected health information to notify or assist in notifying a family member, personal representative or any other person that is responsible for your care of your location, general condition or death. Finally, we may use or disclose your protected health information to an authorized public or private entity to assist in disaster relief efforts and to coordinate uses and disclosures to family or other individuals involved in your healthcare.

**Other Permitted and Required Uses and Disclosures That May Be Made Without Your Authorization or Opportunity to Object**

We may use or disclose your protected health information without your authorization in the following situations:

**Required By Law**:  We may use or disclose your protected health information to the extent that the use or disclosure is required by law. The use or disclosure will be made in compliance with the law and will be limited to the relevant requirements of the law. You will be notified, as required by law, of any such uses or disclosures.

**Public Health:** We may disclose your protected health information for public health activities and purposes to a public health authority that is permitted by law to collect or receive the information. The disclosure will be made for the purpose of controlling disease, injury or disability. We may also disclose your protected health information, if directed by the public health authority, to a foreign government agency that is collaborating with the public health authority.

**Communicable Diseases:** We may disclose your protected health information, if authorized by law, to a person who may have been exposed to a communicable disease or may otherwise be at risk of contracting or spreading the disease or condition.

Health Oversight: We may disclose protected health information to a health oversight agency for activities authorized by law, such as audits, investigations and inspections. Oversight agencies seeking this information include government agencies that oversee the healthcare system, government benefit programs, other government regulatory programs and civil rights laws.

**Abuse or Neglect**: We may disclose your protected health information to a public health authority that is authorized by law to receive reports of abuse or neglect. In addition, we may disclose your protected health information to the governmental entity or agency authorized to receive such information if we believe that you have been a victim of abuse, neglect or domestic violence. In this case, the disclosure will be made consistent with the requirements of applicable federal and state laws.

**Food and Drug Administration**: We may disclose your protected health information to a person or company required by the Food and Drug Administration to; report adverse events, product defects or problems, biologic product deviations, track products; to enable product recalls; to make repairs or replacements or to conduct post marketing surveillance, as required.

**Legal Proceedings**: We may disclose protected health information in the course of any judicial or administrative proceeding, in response to an order of a court or administrative tribunal (to the extent such disclosure is expressly authorized), in certain conditions in response to a subpoena, discovery request or other lawful process.

**Law Enforcement**: We may disclose protected health information so long as applicable legal requirements are met, for law enforcement purposes. These law enforcement purposes include (1) legal processes and those otherwise required by law (2) limited information requests for identification and location purposes (3) pertaining to victims of a crime (4) suspicion that death has occurred as a result of criminal conduct (5) in the event that a crime occurs on the premises of (YOUR COMPANY NAME) and (6) medical emergency (not on (YOUR COMPANY NAME)' premises) and it is likely that a crime has occurred.

**Research**: We may disclose your protected health information to researchers when their research has been approved by an institutional review board that has reviewed the research proposal and established protocols to ensure the privacy of your protected health information.

**Criminal Activity**: Consistent with applicable federal and state laws, we may disclose your protected health information if we believe that the use or disclosure is necessary to prevent or lessen a serious and imminent threat to the health or safety of a person or the public. We may also disclose protected health information if it is necessary for law enforcement authorities to identify or apprehend an individual.

**Military Activity and National Security**: When the appropriate conditions apply, we may use or disclose protected health information of individuals who are Armed Forces personnel (1) for activities deemed necessary by appropriate military command authorities (2) for the purpose of a determination by the Department of Veterans Affairs of your eligibility for benefits or (3) to foreign military authority if you are a member of that foreign military services.

We may also disclose your protected health information to authorized federal officials for conducting national security and intelligence activities, including for the provision of protective services to the president or others legally authorized.

Worker's Compensation: Your protected health information may be disclosed by us as authorized to comply with worker's compensation laws and other similar legally established programs.

**Required Uses and Disclosures**: Under the law, we must make disclosures to you, and when required by the Secretary of the Department of Health and Human Services to investigate or determine our compliance with the requirements of Section 164.500 et.seq., Privacy of Individually Identifiable Health Information.

## YOUR RIGHTS

Following is a statement of your rights with respect to your protected health information and a brief description of how you may exercise these rights.

You have the right to inspect and copy your protected health information. This means you may inspect and obtain a copy of protected health information about you that is contained in a designated record set for as long as we maintain the protected health information.

A "designated record set" contains medical and billing records and any other records that your healthcare provider and (YOUR COMPANY NAME) use for making decisions about you. Under federal law, however, you may not inspect or copy the following records; psychotherapy notes; information compiled in reasonable anticipation of, or use in, a civil, criminal or administrative action or proceeding and protected health information that is subject to law that prohibits access to protected health information. Depending on the circumstances, a decision to deny access may be reviewable. Please contact our Medical Records Department if you have questions about access to your medical record. If you request a copy of the information, we may charge a fee for the costs of retrieving, copying, mailing and any other supplies associated with your request.

You have the right to request a restriction of your protected health information.  This means you may ask us not to use or disclose any part of your protected health information for the purposes of treatment, payment or healthcare operations. You may also request that any part of your protected health information not be disclosed to family members or friends who may be involved in your care or for notification purposes as described in the Notice of Privacy Practices. Your request must state the specific restriction requested and to whom you want the restriction to apply. Your healthcare provider is not required to agree to restrictions you may request. If the healthcare provider believes it is in your best interest to permit use and disclosure of your protected health information, your protected health information will not be restricted.

If your healthcare provider does agree to the requested restriction, we may not use or disclose your protected health information in violation of that restriction unless it is needed to provide emergency treatment. With this in mind, please discuss any restriction you wish to request with your healthcare provider. You may request a restriction by completing a Request Restriction form provided by your healthcare provider.

You have the right to request to receive confidential communication from us by alternative means or at an alternative location.

You have the right to request that we communicate with you about medical matters in a certain way or at a certain location. We will accommodate reasonable requests. We may also condition this accommodation by asking you for information as to how payment will be handled or specification of an alternative address or other method of contact. We will not request an explanation from you as to the basis for the request. Please make this request in writing to our Medical Records Department.

You may have the right to have your healthcare provider amend your protected health information. This means you may request an amendment of protected health information about you in a designated record set for as long as we maintain this information. In certain cases, we may deny your request for an amendment. If we deny your request for amendment, you have the right to file a statement of disagreement with us and we may prepare a rebuttal to your statement and will provide you with a copy of any such rebuttal. Please contact our Medical Records Department to determine if you have a question about amending your medical record.

You have the right to receive an accounting of certain disclosures we have made, if any, of your protected health information. This right applies to disclosures for purposes other than treatment, payment or healthcare operations as described in this Notice of Privacy Practices. It excludes disclosures we may have made to you, for a facility directory, to family members or friends involved in your care, or for notification purposes. You have the right to receive specific information regarding these disclosures that occurred after April 14, 2003. You may request a shorter time frame. The right to receive this information is subject to certain exceptions, restrictions and limitations.

You have the right to a copy of this notice. You may ask us to give you a copy of this notice at any time. To request a copy of this notice, you must make your request in writing to the Privacy Officer.

**COMPLAINTS**

You may file a complaint with us or with the Secretary of Health and Human

Services if you believe your privacy rights have been violated by us. You may file a complaint with us by notifying the Compliance Manager of your complaint at 800-496-5993. We will not retaliate against you for filing a complaint.

I, _____ have been given a copy of (Your Company Name)

 Notice of Privacy Practices and understand how my confidential Information will be shared, as necessary, with employees within the company, and protected by HIPAA regulations.

_____          _____

Name                                                          Date

# CHAPTER 12

# Glossary

ADA Americans with disabilities

ADL'S    Activities of Daily Living (core activities such as bathing, dressing and walking)

AL    Assisted Living – Residence that provides meals and light assistance, the client must be able to evacuate the facility independently to live there

CHF Congestive heart failure

CHR    Chore Services (mowing the lawn, washing walls, etc)

CM    Case Manager (If they are a nurse it may be abbreviated NCM)

CNA    Certified Nursing Assistant, a person who has completed a specific training to be able to provide personal care

CVA Cerebral Vascular Accident (Stroke)

DM    Diabetes mellitus

DX    Diagnosis

DZ    Disease

ERS    Emergency Response Services

ESRD     End stage renal disease

FWW     Front wheeled walker

FX    Fracture

HCBS    Home and Community Based Services – usually paid for under
        Medicaid Aging Waiver

HHA     Home Health Aide (usually similar to a CNA)

HM Home maker – trained to clean and run errands not trained in
personal care

IADL's  Independent Activities of Daily living (activities such as
        balancing a check book and grocery shopping)

ICF   Intermediate Care Facility

Ischemia No blood flow

LTC  long term care (usually thought of as a traditional nursing home)

LTAC     Long Term Acute Care (rehab unit in a hospital)

MI   Myocardial Infarction (Heart attack)

PC       Personal Care (defined as touching the client, bathing, dressing,
         toileting and hygiene activities)

PCA      Personal Care aide, also may be called NA (nursing aid) or CNA if
         they are certified

PRN As needed

SNF  Skilled Nursing Facility

TIA  Transient Ischemic Attack ("Mini" stroke)

# IS A SPECTRUM HOME SERVICES FRANCHISE RIGHT FOR ME?

If after reading this book you decide business ownership is right for you then I suggest you take the next step and begin researching your options. I also invite you to look at owning a Spectrum Home Services franchise.

## THE SPECTRUM HOME SERVICES DIFFERENCE

Spectrum Home Services fills a niche historically ignored by traditional home service companies by providing "Services for All Seasons of Life".
Spectrum Home Services is a home services business with five profit centers:

Senior/Personal Care

Handyman, Cleaning

Yard Care/Snow Removal

Mortgage Field Service

Relocation Services

As a Spectrum Home Services owner you will be involved in networking and building relationships, estimating, hiring and scheduling staff, external advertising and quality checks. Our ideal candidate is someone who can multi-task, has some general management experience, can build relationships on the client end and has some interpersonal skills to develop the employee team. A strong sales background is not necessary.

In the beginning we will have you focus on two of the profit centers of your choice. The following is a brief description of each of the services Spectrum Home Services provides to our clients.

**Companionship** – Social interaction plays a very important role in a happy and healthy life. Sometimes all a senior needs is someone to talk to, eat a meal with or reminisce about family and friends. Our companions are highly trained and are available by the hour, day, or week and we are able to design a package around your specific needs and budget. There are a variety of services available.

**Meal Preparation** – All of the homemaking professionals have food handler permits and are happy to prepare a meal or light snack at the client's request. We can prepare meals from food available in the home or purchase necessary items at the client's request

**Shopping/ Errands** – We are able to help develop a grocery list from which to order groceries for delivery or do personal shopping with or without the client. We will pick up, put away the groceries and clean out the client's refrigerator on a routine basis. If needed, the staff can run errands such as picking up medications, dry cleaning, medical equipment or other items.

**Laundry Services** – Dirty laundry and linens are a breeding ground for germs, and can cause medical complications. We provide complete laundry services in the home or off-site to maintain a healthy living environment. As part of this service dirty laundry is washed, beds are made and clothes are folded and put away as directed by the client or family.

**Personal Care** – We use Certified aides to assist with activities of daily living such as, bathing, shaving, toileting, and applying make-up. While the aides are in the home they are happy to provide assistance with other tasks as needed.

**Respite Care** – Caring for the caregiver is quickly being recognized as essential for the health of the client as well as the caregiver. Spectrum Home Services can provide assistance to family members who need some personal time to run errands, go shopping, exercise, or just relax and recharge their batteries. Cleaning, laundry and other services can be provided during this respite time.

**Home Cleaning -** At Spectrum Home Services, we do far more than just light housekeeping. Our homemaking professionals are trained to maximize efficiency while providing a deep and thorough cleaning during each visit. We provide all the necessary cleaners and tools, so there are no hidden costs. All of our cleaning chemicals are professionally mixed and EPA approved to safely kill germs without emitting harmful odors into the home. Our vacuums are equipped with HEPA filters that are designed to remove toxins from the air while the carpets are cleaned.

**Yard Care** – Our yard care division provides mowing, edging, trimming, weeding, spring and fall clean ups, maintenance of sprinkler systems plus removal of trash and other debris from yards. Our staff respects the customer's input and understands that their yard is extremely important to them. During the winter we also provide snow removal services in a timely manner to reduce the risk of falls.

**Maintenance / Repair** – We have maintenance personnel to perform tasks such as installing grab bars, railings, wheelchair ramps, painting, light plumbing, light electrical, carpet cleaning, window washing, sprinkler winterization and additional items around the home that require a handyman.  We are also able to retrofit homes to make them wheelchair accessible.  Bids are no charge.

**Relocation Services** – Sometimes it's necessary for a client to move into an assisted living facility, nursing home or a family member's home.  Spectrum Home Services can assist in moving clients from one location to another.  We pack and move all personal items including furniture and help unpack as needed. Spectrum Home Services provides a low cost, personalized alternative to traditional moving companies.

## MORTGAGE FIELD SERVICES & PROPERTY PRESERVATION

Spectrum Home Services has taken advantage of the booming foreclosure market through multiple resources. Associations with multiple national mortgage field services companies, Property Management Companies and REO Investment Groups have created consistent work for franchisees across the country.

Spectrum Home Services is the only franchise to maintain foreclosed properties!!! Our Corporate office works hard to provide referrals to our franchisees at no cost to them. The Corporate office has a dedicated Director of Business Relations that sole job is to find new business for the franchisees.

## BUSY HOMEOWNERS AND FAMILIES

Time is precious and busy homeowners and families need more of it! Spectrum Home Services offers homeowner's the services necessary to have more time for the things in life that are important. Spectrum's "**One Call Resolves It All**" package of services eliminates the hassle homeowner's face when ordering multiple home services.

People of all ages are demanding convenient, efficient, and affordable home services and Spectrum Home Services is providing these services.

**BABY-BOOMERS & SENIORS**

America's population is aging and the greatest demographic shift in American history is happening now! Baby boomers are turning 60 at the rate of nearly 8,000 a day. Nearly 75% of the Baby Boomers own homes and they are used to purchasing services for their homes.

Because of current and future medical advancements, Baby-boomers and seniors in general are going to be more active later into life. Spectrum Home Services is the only company in the industry that caters to their variety of changing needs.

Spectrum Home Services provides superior home care services to seniors or disabled individuals so they may remain living safely in their home for as long as possible. We focus on providing custom, quality and affordable services to fit the needs of our clients. Spectrum Home Services is the only company able to provide all services to active seniors, now!

A Spectrum Home Services franchise will allow you to take advantage of this booming market and build a senior client base now giving you a 20-25 year head start on the competition that focuses on just homebound and more frail seniors.

**WE SUPPORT YOU**

We understand that starting and running your own business is a big step and takes a lot of time and effort—we've been there! That's the advantage of owning a Spectrum Home Services franchise. We provide the framework and endless support to assist our franchisees in attaining success in owning their own business.

As the owner of a Spectrum Home Services franchise you have the advantage of operating under an established, trusted name. You will learn the ropes from professionals who have already been through the trial and error process.

Becoming a part of the Spectrum Home Services family places you in the enviable position of being a business owner while allowing you to avoid many of the costly mistakes associated with start-up enterprises.

Franchisees receive extensive support and training from the corporate office. Our commitment to your success is unmatched in the industry. However, unlike other companies in our industry that make this same claim, we put our money where our mouth is! No one has a more extensive start up training program than Spectrum Home Services.

**PRE-TRAINING**
From the very beginning we assign you a Pre-Training Coach who will walk you through our extensive 6 week pre-training process. During the pre-training we help you to get all of the necessary items in place before you come to corporate training. When you come home from your training in Salt Lake City you are ready to open your own business and start providing services.

**CORPORATE TRAINING**
We provide all new franchisees with an extensive 50 hours of training at our corporate offices in Salt Lake City that covers everything you will need to know to run your **new Spectrum Home Services business.**

**STEPS TO SUCCESS & FIELD VISIT TRAINING PROGRAM**
In conjunction with the 5-day training you receive at our corporate headquarters, we provide you with our exclusive 12 week "Steps to Success Training Program".

The Steps to Success Training program is a day by day training program that outlines what you will need to be doing to make

your new business a success. We also go one step further and assign you a business coach.
The Business Coach will assist you as you progress through the 12 week program. The business coach will also make two trips to your territory during the Steps to Success program to help guide you through the start up process.

## SPECTRUM UNIVERSITY & SUPPORT CALLS
Once franchisees complete the Steps to Success Training Program we offer continuing support and training through our Spectrum University Program. Enrollment in the Spectrum University Program is free to all franchisees and is encouraged to help you stay competitive in an ever changing market.

We also hold weekly and monthly support calls to provide an open forum to share best practices and new ideas. This has proved very beneficial to our current franchisees.
Should you need any additional support, we are only a phone call away! The support we offer is endless and completely dependent on your needs.

If you are an entrepreneur at heart who has the willingness to follow a proven system, strong management and people skills, and are interested in providing services that will make a difference in your community we would love to have you be part of the Spectrum Home Services family!

For more information please contact SHS Franchising at www.spectrumhomeservices.com or call our toll free phone number- 800-496-5993

## <u>*DISCLAIMER*</u>

*In the event that you apply the information in this book for yourself or your business, which is your right, the author and the publisher assume no responsibility for your actions or results.*

# THE

# END